I0890342

BIBLE PRAYERS FOR MEN

Publications International, Ltd.

Scripture quotations from *The Holy Bible, King James Version*

Images from Shutterstock.com

Copyright © 2025 Publications International, Ltd. All rights reserved. This book may not be reproduced or quoted in whole or in part by any means whatsoever without written permission from:

Louis Weber, CEO
Publications International, Ltd.
8140 Lehigh Avenue
Morton Grove, IL 60053

Permission is never granted for commercial purposes.

ISBN: 978-1-63938-816-5

Manufactured in China.

8 7 6 5 4 3 2 1

Let's get social!

@Publications_International

@PublicationsInternational

www.pilbooks.com

TABLE OF CONTENTS

INTRODUCTION

Prayers for Men offers prayers, Bible verses, and quotations for a broad spectrum of situations and experiences men encounter in life. In straightforward, everyday language, these prayers echo the thoughts and feelings that rise up from a man's heart.

You may choose to read the book in sequence from cover to cover. Or you can select a quote that best reflects the place in which you find yourself. The prayers are intended to help draw you into dialogue with an ever-present, approachable God, who lovingly calls you into companionship. Individual prayers are brief enough to read in a minute or two, but they'll provide food for thought throughout your day.

Whether *Prayers for Men* becomes a permanent treasure on your personal bookshelf or a book passed among friends, you may be blessed in some way by the role it plays in supporting and strengthening your growing relationship with God.

CHAPTER 1

STRENGTH

The Lord is my light and my salvation; whom shall I fear? the Lord is the strength of my life; of whom shall I be afraid?

–Psalm 27:1

He that hath pity upon the poor lendeth unto the Lord; and that which he hath given will he pay him again.

—Proverbs 19:17

A generosity motivated by strong faith does not go unnoticed. It is always repaid. However, it is not the person to whom we gave who repays us. It is the Lord himself. This frees us from having self-focused expectations or making unreasonable demands. The Lord makes himself our debtor. All that's required of us is our strong sense of belief.

I can do all things through Christ which strengtheneth me.

—Philippians 4:13

My parents' deaths effected a profound transition for me. My mother died when I was 30 years old, and my father died this year, less than two years after we lost Mom. I am an adult, a single dad, and though I have been self-sufficient for years, I deeply miss being able to call my parents for counsel when faced with life's challenges. Mom and Dad were always there to support me and my son Evan. Since their deaths, I have sometimes felt alone as I've tried to navigate the challenges of parenting and make decisions about the future. Just last week, I met with my financial planner to adjust the college savings plan I am pursuing for my son. I so wished I could call Dad to talk through the options. But I prayed about it, and slept on it, and when I woke the next morning, I had a decision made and felt at peace.

God, you are there: please help me to remember this, and that my strength to face life's trials comes from you.

The Lord will give strength unto his people; the Lord will bless his people with peace.

–Psalm 29:11

God strengthens individuals, but he also strengthens groups. This thought gave me comfort last night as I prepared for a summer mission trip. I will be traveling to Oklahoma to help rebuild homes destroyed in a tornado, and have been charged with directing eight college-aged kids from my church. I am a skilled carpenter but less certain about leading a group.

God, I pray you will grant my team the strength and cohesiveness we need to do our jobs well.

Fear thou not; for I am with thee: be not dismayed; for I am thy God: I will strengthen thee; yea, I will help thee; yea, I will uphold thee with the right hand of my righteousness.

–Isaiah 41:10

As a cop, I am used to handling trouble. I like to think of myself as pretty unflappable, and my family and friends look to me when they are afraid. But last week, my teenage son was involved in an auto accident, and when I got the call, it was still unclear as to whether there were any fatalities. I was filled with fear as my wife and I drove quickly to the hospital. What if our son didn't make it? What if he lived but had sustained brain damage? My wife and I held hands as we sped through the night streets, and began to pray out loud. God, you were there with us, in our car; you got us to the hospital emergency room safely; you were there when the doctor told us our son's legs had been shattered in the accident, but that he will live. Our boy's road to recovery will be long. We still don't know if he'll ever walk again without aid. It is a hard time for our family, but God, you have always been there for us. Whatever lies ahead, we will not make this journey alone. Please help me to remember, on days when I falter, that your strength is the ultimate antidote to fear.

> *Jesus saith unto him, Rise, take up thy bed, and walk.*
>
> –John 5:8

Sometimes I am afraid. Sometimes the path before me seems almost impossible. Last year, I decided to return to school. The office where I work indicated that I would have a better chance of advancing if I pursued a graduate degree. But I was anxious. School has never come easily to me, and at this stage of my life, I have myriad responsibilities, including a house and two active children under the age of five. But I prayed about it, and worked with my wife to figure out a humane course schedule that makes sense for our family. Though it will take a long time, I will eventually earn my degree. This first year I have been gratified to learn that I can keep up with my coursework and still make time for my job and family. It isn't always easy, though, and I pray for strength every day. I have learned that if I have faith, God will help me take on enormous challenges.

> *Be strong and of a good courage, fear not, nor be afraid of them: for the Lord thy God, he it is that doth go with thee; he will not fail thee, nor forsake thee.*
>
> –Deuteronomy 31:6

God, there are times when we must be brave and face an adversary. I work at an ad agency and we are currently bidding on some client work. I'll be making a presentation and competing against rival firms for a lucrative account. Sometimes the competition can get cutthroat. The main challenger has a reputation for badmouthing the competition, and I'm not looking forward to interacting with this gentleman the day of the presentations.

God, please strengthen me so that I might face my rival with grace.

Labour not for the meat which perisheth, but for that meat which endureth unto everlasting life, which the Son of man shall give unto you: for him hath God the Father sealed.

—John 6:27

Heavenly Father, I seek the nourishment that comes from true inner strength. I know that food fuels the body, but my spirit needs the fuel of deep and abiding peace and the understanding that I'm never alone in the world. With you, Father, I have that foundation of strength to feed me from the inside out. I'm able to go forth and face any challenge and overcome any obstacle. I ask that you continue to nourish me with resilience, fortitude, and faith.

I will love thee, O Lord, my strength. The Lord is my rock, and my fortress, and my deliverer; my God, my strength, in whom I will trust; my buckler, and the horn of my salvation, and my high tower.

–Psalm 18:1–2

Rock, fortress, deliverer, shield, horn, tower: wow, that's a lot! But God's strength is all of these. If you need a place to stand today, or a place to hide, your trust in God is more than sufficient to protect you and encourage you. Any one of these would be enough, but you get them all. Because the Lord is your strength.

They that wait upon the Lord shall renew their strength; they shall mount up with wings as eagles; they shall run, and not be weary; and they shall walk, and not faint.

–Isaiah 40:31

O Lord, nothing drains us of our strength more completely than grief. But in times of sorrow, you come alongside us and give us strength to do things we never thought possible. Thus distraught family members are able to make final arrangements, deliver eloquent eulogies, and rise above their grief to do whatever needs to be done. We know that's your strength carrying us in those times, Lord. The promises in your Word give us hope. Your grace abounds in a special way to those who mourn. We praise you for your mercy, Lord. We thank you for your strength.

Wait on the Lord: be of good courage, and he shall strengthen thine heart: wait, I say, on the Lord.

—Psalm 27:14

Lord, thank you for calling me to yourself and then giving me your Spirit to strengthen me—heart, soul, mind, and body—to work in ways that bring honor to you. This goal of being a model of good works in every respect makes me realize how much I need you each moment. And as I grow in a life of doing what is right and true and good, help me grow in humility as well, remembering that you are the source of my strength.

And Moses called unto Joshua, and said unto him in the sight of all Israel, Be strong and of a good courage: for thou must go with this people unto the land which the Lord hath sworn unto their fathers to give them; and thou shalt cause them to inherit it.

—Deuteronomy 31:7

David's mother, Olivia, had always been the matriarch, the "glue" that held her family together. When Olivia was diagnosed with Parkinson's disease, David, as the eldest of his siblings, knew he needed to step up and be strong for everyone. "I suddenly was called upon to mediate and make decisions that affected the entire family," David remembers. "It was ultimately a time of growth, but I felt challenged. I prayed for guidance and strength a lot."

Dear God, give me strength. Please embolden me to be a leader, just as Moses uplifted Joshua to lead the Israelites into the promised land.

And Joshua said unto them, Fear not, nor be dismayed, be strong and of good courage: for thus shall the Lord do to all your enemies against whom ye fight.

–Joshua 10:25

God, teach me to not fear adversity. It is a father's kneejerk reaction to protect his children from all trials, but one cannot travel through life without reversals of fortune. Help me to accept and face challenges not only to myself but to my children. My kids will face unkindness; they will face unfairness, loss, and even cruelty in their life's journey. God, help me to remember that adversity breeds character–that we cannot necessarily control what happens to us but we can control our response to it. Grant me the strength to respond to adversity with grace, and please guide me as I give my children the tools to greet life's vicissitudes with faith in you, and with courage.

CHAPTER 2
PRAISE

I will praise thee, O Lord, with my whole heart; I will shew forth all thy marvellous works. I will be glad and rejoice in thee: I will sing praise to thy name, O thou most High.

–Psalm 9:1–2

And hath made us kings and priests unto God and his Father; to him be glory and dominion for ever and ever. Amen.

—Revelation 1:6

I am an editor by trade and a fiction writer by choice. For the past several years, I have been working on a novel in the evening and on weekends. Yesterday I made final touches on what I believe is the final draft. I closed my laptop, pulled on my jacket, and went for a long walk. It was almost hard to believe that the project that has consumed my free time for so long was complete. I felt a strange mix of relief and exhilaration, and experienced a great welling of praise in my heart.

Lord, you have been with me every step of the way, even when things seemed unclear as to how to proceed with this book. Now it is done! Thank you, thank you, for being there. Thank you for helping me to accomplish this.

I will praise the name of God with a song, and will magnify him with thanksgiving.

–Psalm 69:30

My daughter Alexa, a high school student, loves to sing. She has been involved in choir since she was a little girl. Yesterday was Monday, and my daughter came home from school discouraged about a misunderstanding with a friend, and the fact that she had more homework than she'd anticipated. Every Monday evening is rehearsal time for the church choir Alexa is in. The kids meet for an hour or so to practice right after dinner. Usually she looks forward to it, but yesterday she didn't want to go. She felt tired and worried about her schoolwork. I encouraged her to go anyway, and promised that I'd be right there at the end of practice, ready to bring her back home. When I dropped my girl off, she looked positively glum. Imagine my surprise when I picked up a beaming, transformed daughter an hour later! "I can't believe I always forget how good this choir makes me feel!" Alexa enthused, and I had to smile.

Lord, thank you for reminding me and my beloved daughter how praising you in song can uplift one's heart.

And God said, Let there be lights in the firmament of the heaven to divide the day from the night; and let them be for signs, and for seasons, and for days, and years.

—Genesis 1:14

Thank you for astronomical wonders. Solar and lunar eclipses, harvest moons, times when a planet is very clearly visible, meteor showers—they all provoke wonder in your creation. Staring up at the sky, I am aware of how small I am, and how grand your works. And even when I am alone, I know others are looking up at the same sky and experiencing that same awe.

But I will hope continually, and will yet praise thee more and more.

—Psalm 71:14

My old college friend Tom is an artist. He lives in a city near my home, and occasionally he'll have a gallery showing of his work downtown. I always try to make his shows, and we usually also manage to get together for a meal every month or so. His shows are a perfect time for me to compliment his work. But one evening when we were just meeting for dinner, I mentioned how impressed I am by a series of sculptures he's been making from pressed wood. Even though I had already praised that same work at a recent show, the innovative nature of the work has stayed with me, and I wanted to share that. Tom was uplifted by my comment. It turns out he'd had a frustrating day in the studio and my admiration, coming from out of the blue like that, meant a lot to him. The experience reminded me that praise is not a one-time thing—you never know when another person might be struggling, or how much repeating a kind word can mean.

God, may I remember to praise others even as I praise you, again and again.

By him therefore let us offer the sacrifice of praise to God continually, that is, the fruit of our lips giving thanks to his name.

—Hebrews 13:15

After a routine dental procedure went awry, Jose became very ill. He contracted blood poisoning and the pain in his jaw was beyond anything she'd ever experienced. Thanks to antibiotics and sound medical care, Jose recovered, but now, even months later, when he wakes pain-free he still gives thanks to God. "It took an extreme situation to remind me of the importance of thanking God; being grateful inspires joy, and I feel closer to God than ever," Jose says.

Dear Lord, I understand how important it is to give thanks to you. It draws me closer to you, and is good for my heart.

Let them praise thy great and terrible name; for it is holy.

–Psalm 99:3

I try not to swear in front of my children, but the other day, while attempting to fix a few loose boards, I hit my thumb, not the fence, with my hammer. I took the Lord's name in vain and howled a few other choice epithets while hopping in pain around the backyard. My two little daughters were playing nearby, which meant I had to do some apologizing after the fact. "Dad spoke God's name in anger–not cool," I began. I explained how a name is a profound thing. "It would feel bad if I yelled your name in an angry way, wouldn't it?" I asked the girls. They nodded their heads vigorously. "God doesn't like it when you yell his name either, does he?" my littlest asked. "God's name is powerful and holy," I said, hugging her. "It should be said with praise." At that point, I decided the fence could wait, and we went out for ice cream. But the conversation stayed with me.

Lord, when I say your name, may it always be with proper reverence.

My lips shall utter praise, when thou hast taught me thy statutes.

—Psalm 119:171

In a church or family, praising can have the nice effect of building up others and spreading cheer. In our house, we'll occasionally indulge in what we call "love bombardment": someone will get singled out for a blitz of praise, during which everyone else in the house heaps compliments upon the designated recipient. We usually focus on someone who's had a long or challenging day. It doesn't take long for everyone to be caught up in laughter, and the object of affection gets a nice boost. Everyone needs a lift sometimes, and taking part in praise bombardment has proven, in our house at least, to be a balm for all concerned.

Dear Lord, help me to remember that attitudes are infectious.

Let the heaven and earth praise him, the seas, and every thing that moveth therein.

—Psalm 69:34

Today I thank you for the beautiful, often mysterious creatures of the seas and oceans. From the intricate ecosystems of tide pools to the massive forms of blue whales, you created it all! I wonder if the joy of dolphins as they flip and spin and play is their way of singing praise to you? I praise you for the marvels of our world!

Now to that God, who has suffered so much for us, who at one giving has conferred on us so many good things, and will yet confer so many more, to this God let every creature who is in heaven or upon the earth, in the sea or in the depth of the abyss, render praise, glory, honor and blessing. He is himself our virtue and our strength. He alone is good, lofty, almighty, admirable, and glorious; the only holy, worthy of praise and blessed through ages of ages. Amen.

—St. Francis of Assisi

> *Give unto the Lord, ye kindreds of the people, give unto the Lord glory and strength. Give unto the Lord the glory due unto his name: bring an offering, and come before him: worship the Lord in the beauty of holiness.*
>
> –1 Chronicles 16:28–29

The greatest offering we can bring to God is praise. Our worship is about this, praise for his glory, strength, name, and beauty. Pause to reflect on the greatness of God today. Then say it out loud: Lord, you are worthy of my praise. Make this your offering today: lips that praise him and a heart that treasures him, awed by his holiness and content with his love. Add more to the list and worship God.

I might not be able to praise you with an instrument, Lord, but I can still thank you for your faithfulness.

When I'm making home repairs, I can praise you for the roof over my head. When I'm stuck in traffic, I can praise you for the beautiful scenery around me. When I'm fighting illness, I can praise you for the Spirit you breathed into me. And when the people I love struggle, I can praise you for bringing such wonderful people into my life.

This gift of life is precious, and I know my eternity is secure in you. Though my days are not always easy, I know that you stay faithfully by my side—guiding my steps and filling my heart with joy.

I praise you with all the resources at my disposal, Lord. I know that you treasure the motive of my praise—not the means.

CHAPTER 3

WORK AND LEADERSHIP

And let the beauty of the Lord our God be upon us: and establish thou the work of our hands upon us; yea, the work of our hands establish thou it.

–Psalm 90:17

And whatsoever ye do, do it heartily, as to the Lord, and not unto men.

–Colossians 3:23

I have always liked the expression, "You aren't the boss of me!" I'm an independent person, I run my own business, and I like being in control. And yet, sometimes I need to be reminded that there is someone I'm answerable to, and that someone is God. God asks that I be accountable in my actions, in the choices I make, and in the example I set for others, at home and in the world. I try to live my life with abandon, and when I keep God's Word first and foremost in my thinking, I find I can live fully in a way that feels good.

God, you are my ultimate boss and I thank you!

For which of you, intending to build a tower, sitteth not down first, and counteth the cost, whether he have sufficient to finish it?

–Luke 14:28

My wife Meg and I recently bought our first house, a little brick bungalow with beautiful bay windows. We've lived in apartments up until now, and suddenly we are homeowners, with all that entails: a postage-stamp-sized yard, a room we can use as an office, and even a guest room. It's been exciting to transform the little bungalow from a house into our home, and we've spent time and money in our efforts to do so. There are the practical purchases, like a small lawn mower, and then there are what Meg and I call "fun" purchases, like new curtains for the living room. There are many more things we'd like to do–the current light fixture in the dining room is pretty ugly, for instance, and we'd like to replace it–but we work hard for our income, and know we need to pace ourselves financially. As Meg reminded me the other day, God instructs us to plan carefully down to the last detail, and calculate the costs of everything we do. The new light fixture is going to have to wait, but in the meantime, we are wise to be happy with the fruits of our labors–the blessing of a new home.

Though he were a Son, yet learned he obedience by the things which he suffered.

–Hebrews 5:8

Obedience is a tricky concept. We don't hear as much about it in these modern days! We prize leadership, sometimes at the expense of being a good team member. When I am in a group, at work or at church or at another activity, help me not value leadership so much that I don't appreciate the work every team member does. And when I am in a leadership role, help me remember to be obedient to your will and your words. Let me follow the model of Jesus.

And Moses said unto God, Who am I, that I should go unto Pharaoh, and that I should bring forth the children of Israel out of Egypt?

–Exodus 3:11

My uncle, the president of a paper company, used to paraphrase Shakespeare and say, "Heavy is the head that wears the crown." I was a child at the time and didn't really understand what he was talking about. Now that I am an adult and hold a leadership position at work, I think I have an idea of what Shakespeare and my uncle might had been saying. I have many employees looking to me for guidance, advice, and a secure livelihood. Sometimes, when we are dealing with difficult clients or getting pressure from shareholders, I question whether I am fit to lead. I must remind myself: even Moses had doubts, and God strengthens us.

Dear Lord, thank you for giving me the grit and wisdom to effectively direct those who look to me for leadership.

Let him that stole steal no more: but rather let him labour, working with his hands the thing which is good, that he may have to give to him that needeth.

—Ephesians 4:28

My 14-year-old son Cal began high school this year. He's always run with a nice group of kids, but this year he drifted into a new crowd and my wife and I were dismayed to see some changes in his behavior. He stopped taking his schoolwork seriously and his grades dropped. Cal's attitude at home became blasé and sullen. It seemed to be "cool" to not care about school or his family. Worried about the threat of drugs and alcohol, my wife and I tried various things, from grounding our son and withdrawing privileges to encouraging him to join a club at school. But it was only when my dad introduced Cal to woodworking that we saw some of the old Cal return. Working creatively with his hands seems almost therapeutic for our son. He likes going over to my dad's workshop. He likes creating something that lasts. Cal hasn't been hanging out as much with the new group of friends. He's working on a series of bookshelves for his room.

God, thank you for helping us to help Cal. Finding constructive things to do is a great way to re-channel energy that's been misspent.

Come unto me, all ye that labour and are heavy laden, and I will give you rest.

–Matthew 11:28

I run my own business, and while I appreciate the many perks of my lifestyle–working from home, a flexible schedule, being my own boss–I sometimes find myself burning the midnight oil and working too hard in an effort to "keep up." The other night I found myself awake, crunching numbers, well into the early hours of the morning. Those dark hours can be lonely ones. As I wrapped up for the night and put my calculator aside, I felt worn out–not just physically, but emotionally. But as I made my way up the stairs to bed, I thought about Christ's promise of giving rest to the weary, and I was comforted. "I'm too tired to do anything more," I thought and, giving over the day's work to Jesus, slept well.

God, thank you for the gift of your son, who is there for us to share our burden and restore us with rest.

Miserably, embarrassingly, and very publicly, Lord, I failed at work, costing the company money and time. Peers sympathize but are mostly relieved they didn't blunder. Remind me not to gloat the next time I am successful and someone else wears the dunce cap of failure. Help me separate what went wrong from who went wrong, for my efforts were well-intended. Be with me as I walk down the hall, chin up, face forward to try again. Help me learn from my failures, and first of all not to believe that I am one.

As I go through this day, help me to be sensitive to the fears and cares of my fellow workers. Remind me not to add my grievances and burdens to their own.

–Anonymous

Lord, we pray for all those in positions of leadership in our government. The pressures and influences on them are of a magnitude we can only imagine. Watch over them, Lord. Reach out to them with your grace, and instill in them your character, your priorities, and your vision for our country and our world.

Happy is he that hath the God of Jacob for his help, whose hope is in the Lord his God: Which made heaven, and earth, the sea, and all that therein is: which keepeth truth for ever.

–Psalm 146:5-6

Bless our work, Lord of vineyards and seas. We long to leave a mark as visible as a building or bridge. We yearn to be connected with what we do and to do something that matters. Show us that what we do is as indelible as a hand-print on fresh concrete even though our mark may be in spots no one can see right now except us. Harvest comes in its own sweet time. Bless our left-behind marks, for with you as our foundation, our work is as essential to the overall structure of life as a concrete pillar.

He that walketh with wise men shall be wise: but a companion of fools shall be destroyed.

–Proverbs 13:20

This proverb reminds me of the balance that is necessary in life, Lord. Often I am the one learning from the wisdom and experience of others, but help me to stand tall and be a leader when a situation warrants it. Help me to give a good example and to be mindful of the company I keep. I am not here to judge, but I do want to keep company with those who are using their time on this earth in constructive rather than wasteful ways. Help me to heed the advice of those with more life experience and–when called–to lead with a strong, gentle example.

Thank you for employment. I may not enjoy all aspects of my job, but I'm grateful for the financial security it offers. I'm grateful for the dignity of work, for my conscientious colleagues, and for those days when I feel like I'm getting to use my God-given talents to the full!

I ask your blessings today on those looking for employment, that you give them a spirit of hope and patience as they wait for the right work to come along.

The integrity of the upright shall guide them: but the perverseness of transgressors shall destroy them.

–Proverbs 11:3

We have been guilty, Lord, of looking for our leaders only in the places of wealth and influence. We confess a fascination with power. We want to glorify the outwardly successful, passing over those who have learned to live wisely and with true integrity. Rather, we tend to follow after those who give blithe answers with the appearance of absolute confidence.

But you have offered us better, we know.

Your plan for us is that we follow leaders guided by the right and the good. Your spirit fills those who walk in humility, patience, and self-sacrifice. Please open our eyes that we may see those gentle faces beckoning us upward and onward in a spirit of love. They are all around us, we're certain. Only open our eyes!

All work can be good, Lord, for you can upgrade the most mundane, difficult, or nerve-wracking job into one that matters. God of all skills and vocations, bless and inspire my work; deliver me from boredom and laziness.

Blessed is he who has found his work; let him ask no other blessedness. He has a work, a life-purpose; he has found it and will follow it.

–Thomas Carlyle

CHAPTER 4

FORGIVENESS

Forbearing one another, and forgiving one another, if any man have a quarrel against any: even as Christ forgave you, so also do ye.

–Colossians 3:13

Then Peter said unto them, Repent, and be baptized every one of you in the name of Jesus Christ for the remission of sins, and ye shall receive the gift of the Holy Ghost.

—Acts 2:38

When we forgive, our hearts are lightened. It has taken me much of my adult life to understand that basic premise. And even now, I can approach forgiveness from the standpoint of the gift I'm giving another. It is only after I have forgiven someone, and my spirit lifts, that I remember, again: I benefit as much, if not more, than the person I've pardoned.

Dear Lord, thank you for the gift you give freely each time I am moved to absolve another. Thank you for rewarding forgiveness by enriching my heart spiritually.

And when ye stand praying, forgive, if ye have ought against any: that your Father also which is in heaven may forgive you your trespasses.

–Mark 11:25

When my dear wife died of cancer, many friends stepped forward, but some–even friends I hold dear–disappointed me by not being there for me as much as I might have hoped. Death is a frightening thing, my wife's death was untimely, and I tried to remember that people's lives are complex. Sometimes, I imagine, my expectations were simply too high. And yet it was painful for me to understand that some loved ones could not, for whatever reason, be there for me in my grief. It was only through prayer that I gained a measure of relief, perspective, and calm.

God, thank you for always being there to listen to me. Prayer puts me in the right frame of mind to forgive others and, sometimes, to forgive myself.

In whom we have redemption through his blood, the forgiveness of sins, according to the riches of his grace.

—Ephesians 1:7

Some days are better than others. Yesterday I was patient when my son forgot his books at school (again), when a coworker slighted me, and when I got the wrong change at the movie theater. Some days we are invited to forgive, and forgive again, and we can rise to the challenge. But there can be another kind of day, when I feel my temper rising and my brow lowering. On those days, I try to remember the fact that God has no reason to forgive us and yet he does so, again and again. He chooses to do so because of his grace.

Dear Lord, may I always remember that forgiveness is a gift from you, and may I likewise, through your grace, be reminded to exercise forgiveness, joyfully, in my own affairs.

And forgive us our debts, as we forgive our debtors.

—Matthew 6:12

In quarrels with family members or friends, I am usually quick to forgive and move on; life is too short for grudges! And yet, one area in which forgiveness does not come so easily for me is a pardon of debt. I recently loaned money to a friend, and he has been almost cavalier about paying me back; though we agreed he would repay me in full by last week, he has not done so. I am surprised at how much the situation bothers me, but it was a considerable sum. I see my friend at work, and these last few days, though he seems unconcerned, I have found myself struggling to stay positive and gracious when we are together. It's uncomfortable to bring up, but I know I must talk with him about the loan.

God, please grant me the serenity and wisdom to approach this sensitive matter with grace. Teach me how to forgive my friend if he cannot repay me as quickly or completely as I might have hoped.

For by grace are ye saved through faith; and that not of yourselves: it is the gift of God.

–Ephesians 2:8

I am grateful that you don't require spiritual gymnastics from me when I sin, Lord. You just call me to come to you with a humble and repentant heart. In my pride I sometimes want to do something that will impress you—something that will "make up for it" somehow. But you just shake your head and keep calling me to humble myself and bring my sincere sorrow to you. That often doesn't seem like enough to me. But I guess that's the point: I can never earn your grace; it is a gift. Christ died on the cross for us because it is beyond our powers to make up for all the sins we have committed. I bring my contrite heart before you now, Lord. Thank you for receiving it as an acceptable sacrifice.

Then came Peter to him, and said, Lord, how oft shall my brother sin against me, and I forgive him? till seven times? Jesus saith unto him, I say not unto thee, Until seven times: but, Until seventy times seven.

–Matthew 18:21–22

My aging parents have required more support in the last year or so, and my brother and I have tried to work together to meet their needs. Most of the time we succeed, but in the past few months, we have started butting heads. Part of our disagreements simply stem from the stress of our current circumstances. Both our parents are very ill and usually conflict occurs when I need to put the needs of my own children first. My brother, who doesn't have a wife or family, doesn't always understand when I need to juggle my caregiving roles. I do the best I can, but I recently found out that my brother has been complaining about me to other family members behind my back. I felt hurt and betrayed. I wish he had come to me to resolve our differences.

When I confronted him, we had a heated exchange. I didn't receive an apology, and while I assured him I understood and that we would just move on, I have held bitterness in my heart. That resentment has been eating away at me. Yesterday my wife sat me down. She had guessed at my struggle, and counseled me that if ever there was a time for forgiveness, this was it. My brother and I need one another as we cope with the needs of our parents, and the anger I've been harboring is corrosive to my health and spirit.

Dear God, please help me to forgive those who I feel have betrayed me. Please help me move forward with a spirit of grace.

Judge not, and ye shall not be judged: condemn not, and ye shall not be condemned: forgive, and ye shall be forgiven.

–Luke 6:37

Dear God, why is it often the people closest to us that hurt us the most? Today I ask for the strength to deal with difficult people in the way you would want me to. Today I ask for the ability to find it in my heart to forgive them their trespasses, as I would hope they'd forgive mine. Today I ask for enough love to look beyond their problems and see them as you see them, as human beings deserving of love and care, even if I have to do it from a distance. Help me to forgive and move on, God. Amen.

From that time Jesus began to preach, and to say, Repent: for the kingdom of heaven is at hand.

—Matthew 4:17

Lord, I never want to think about my failures. But I know I need to acknowledge my sins—not to wallow in guilt, but to repent and then let go of them. Thank you for holding out your arms in forgiveness. It is a gift, that you know my shortcomings and love me anyway. You want me to repent so that you can welcome me into the kingdom!

If we confess our sins, he is faithful and just to forgive us our sins, and to cleanse us from all unrighteousness.

—1 John 1:9

First we have to confess. This is not easy. Pride sometimes gets in the way. It is hard to admit we have done wrong. And sometimes humility gets in the way too. It is hard to feel we are worthy. And indeed we are not.

Fortunately, forgiveness depends on our Father's faithfulness and not our own. And it depends on his justice, since our sins are paid for in Christ. In this way he chooses to forgive. Better yet, he chooses to cleanse our sin, gradually but surely taking away the desires and weaknesses that caused us to fail in the first place. He is willing and able to change those who confess. And he does change them because he is faithful and just.

Blessed is he whose transgression is forgiven, whose sin is covered. Blessed is the man unto whom the Lord imputeth not iniquity, and in whose spirit there is no guile.

–Psalm 32:1–2

Dear Lord, I've been able to forgive others who have hurt me, but why can't I forgive myself? I've made so many bad choices in life, and now I feel as though they're catching up with me. I know that you forgive me of any transgressions, but please help me today to let go of the regret and sorrow over things I didn't do right, and choices I made in haste. Help me release the grip of anger for my sins, because it's only serving to make me unhappy and sick inside. I long to be set free of the past, and face a fresh future with you beside me to guide my ways. Help me forgive the one person in my life that needs it most—myself. Thank you, Lord. Amen.

Therefore we are buried with him by baptism into death: that like as Christ was raised up from the dead by the glory of the Father, even so we also should walk in newness of life.

–Romans 6:4

Lord, today my heart goes out to all those whose past mistakes weigh them down and make any vision they have of their future dreary at best. Oh, that they might know you and the saving grace you bring! Draw near to them today, Lord. Reveal yourself to them in a way that will reach them, and through your mercy and forgiveness, bestow upon them a new vision—a new hope.

If thou, Lord, shouldest mark iniquities, O Lord, who shall stand? But there is forgiveness with thee, that thou mayest be feared.

—Psalm 130:3–4

Few promises bring as much comfort as this one: there is forgiveness in the Lord. We cannot stand in God's presence, so great is our failure and sin. Like Isaiah we fall on our faces before the holiness of God. We say, "Woe is me! . . . for mine eyes have seen the King, the Lord of hosts" (Isaiah 6:5). And yet there is forgiveness. The seraphim flies from the altar before the throne of God and says, "Thine iniquity is taken away, and thy sin purged" (Isaiah 6:7). What freedom there is in this! And what fear as well. We are awed because "with the Lord there is mercy, and with him is plenteous redemption" (Psalm 130:7). Who could stand if the Lord should mark our iniquities without extending his forgiveness?

CHAPTER 5
AGING

Cast me not off in the time of old age; forsake me not when my strength faileth.

–Psalm 71:9

The glory of young men is their strength: and the beauty of old men is the grey head.

–Proverbs 20:29

Yesterday, I looked in the bathroom mirror and noticed some gray hair near my temples, and even the start of what might be a receding hairline. I've never thought of myself as particularly vain, but these changes took me by surprise. I told my wife over breakfast that I'm not sure I like them! I even wondered aloud if I should darken my hair to mask the signs of aging. But as she reminded me, smiling, "God tells us, don't hide our gray–revel in it!"

God, thank you for reminding me to take joy in every stage of my life.

The righteous shall flourish like the palm tree: he shall grow like a cedar in Lebanon. Those that be planted in the house of the Lord shall flourish in the courts of our God. They shall still bring forth fruit in old age; they shall be fat and flourishing.

–Psalm 92:12–14

When I was a boy, I had a close relationship with my dad's father, a quiet, righteous man who had a little house in northern Michigan. My parents and I would go up to see him every summer, and during our visits, I'd take long walks with my grandfather. We didn't always talk, but we shared one another's company with pleasure. As I became a teen, though, I was drawn more and more to my friends. One summer I told my parents that I didn't want to make the yearly trip. I was old enough to stay home alone, I argued, and preferred to remain behind. I still remember my dad's response: "There will come a day when your grandpa is no longer with us. He has much to offer, and you will be glad of the times you shared when he is gone." I reluctantly agreed. It turned out that visit was an especially good one. My grandfather taught me how to play chess, and though he had started to walk with a cane, we still hiked the property. We enjoyed our usual companionable silence on the walk. I returned home feeling restored.

The following winter, a heart attack took my grandfather's life. To this day, I feel tremendous gratitude that I shared that last special visit with a man whose decency continues to inform who I strive to be.

Hearken unto thy father that begat thee, and despise not thy mother when she is old.

—Proverbs 23:22

Throughout my life I have enjoyed many milestones: attaining a college degree, securing my first job, marriage, the birth of my two children, and just recently, seeing my relationship with my parents flip as they age and begin to rely on me as I once relied on them. Each life chapter has brought its joys and trials, and while it is my privilege to support my mom and dad, I confess that their new vulnerability sometimes fills me with fear, and on my worst days, resentment. My life is so full. My children, in high school now, still need me, perhaps more than ever as they face more adult challenges of their own. Sometimes I feel as though there are not enough hours in the day to work and make sure the needs of my loved ones are met. Sometimes I don't want to face or be present for the way my parents have aged.

God, as I grow older and my life becomes more complicated, please help me to remember to always honor my mother and father. They remain my parents and have much to offer me. May I never forget them or shirk my responsibilities amid the everyday cares of working and parenting.

> *Thou shalt rise up before the hoary head, and honour the face of the old man, and fear thy God: I am the Lord.*
>
> –Leviticus 19:32

I live in a time and society that worship youth: open any magazine and there are ads for products that help us to "stay young and beautiful." We strive for youth even as–perhaps because–we live in a culture that can marginalize elders as irrelevant, or a burden. Unattractive. This attitude sometimes makes me fear aging. I also find myself fighting the impulse to pull back from the elderly people in my life, again, out of fear–fear of their vulnerability, of their bumps and spots and rough places. But God reminds us that when we honor our elders, we honor God.

Dear Lord, help me to keep my heart focused on what matters, not age, or appearance, but the humanity in others, as well as the humanity in myself. Teach me to remember that true beauty comes from where our body and spirit meet.

For which cause we faint not; but though our outward man perish, yet the inward man is renewed day by day.

–2 Corinthians 4:16

I recently turned 50 and have started to see changes in my body. I have had to start watching cholesterol levels. I've had to work harder to stay trim. Sometimes I fear that my mind is not as sharp as it once was. I don't have as great a faculty for remembering things as I did when I was younger, so I rely more on lists to keep the day running smoothly. More and more, conversations with friends circle around to these types of health issues, and sometimes I feel fearful at the prospect of aging. And yet, God reminds us that even when our bodies and minds begin to break down, he renews our spirit.

God, thank you for being with me at every age, in every chapter of my life.

Fear ye not therefore, ye are of more value than many sparrows.

—Matthew 10:31

Harold, a 70-year-old widower, stays active and enjoys a wide circle of friends, his two sons, and his grandkids. But sometimes, his body reminds him of the passage of time. "I have a little arthritis," he admits. "Some days it slows me down; it bothers me when I have to ask my kids for help. But then I remember: I'm still me, even with arthritis. My kids love me. And so does God!"

Dear God, I am growing older. My body is not as strong as it used to be; sometimes I feel like a burden. But you tell us we are valued, always—please help me to remember this!

And even to your old age I am he; and even to hoar hairs will I carry you: I have made, and I will bear; even I will carry, and will deliver you.

—Isaiah 46:4

Lord, today I ask your special blessing on the elderly among us. No matter how old we are, we notice our bodies aging. How difficult it must be to be near the end of life and struggling to hold on to mobility, vision, hearing, and wellness of being. Give us compassion for those older than we are, Lord, and thank you for your promise that you will be with us to the very end of our days.

Children's children are the crown of old men; and the glory of children are their fathers.

—Proverbs 17:6

Lord, time and again I see that you intend for the generations to go through life together. The joy the youngest child brings to the eldest grandparent is such a blessing to all who witness it. Even when it isn't possible for us all to be together all the time, let us see the wisdom in sharing our lives. Please keep us ever alert to the unique gifts each generation has to share.

CHAPTER 6

PRIDE

Better is the end of a thing than the beginning thereof: and the patient in spirit is better than the proud in spirit.

–Ecclesiastes 7:8

God resisteth the proud, and giveth grace to the humble.

–1 Peter 5:5

Dear Lord, it's tempting to look upon my life and feel prideful for all that I have accomplished. But everything I have has come from you, given freely to me because of your grace and not because of my actions. I go to you now in humility, reminded of my weaknesses and sins and thankful for the abundance of gifts you have given me. I am yours, pledged in your Son's holy blood to obey your Word. Amen.

Charity suffereth long, and is kind; charity envieth not; charity vaunteth not itself, is not puffed up.

–1 Corinthians 13:4

Sometimes pride gets the better of me. When things are going well in my life, I am not above indulging in a certain prideful righteousness. Last week at work, I learned I'd earned a significant bonus for my quarterly sales. My first thought was, "Well, I deserve it! I worked harder than anyone else." In fact, I was almost smug. I felt certain that I'd bested Glenn, my coworker; he and I are "friendly rivals" when it comes to sales numbers. But too much pride can be much like eating too much dessert–it might feel good at first, but it can catch up to a person. As the day wore on, I was, I'll confess, almost sick of myself–a little self-congratulation goes a long way, it turns out. I decided to take a walk to clear my head. The neighborhood where I work has some interesting restaurants and shops. I passed a cool new donut shop known for its interesting flavor combinations. Out of curiosity, I stopped to look in. Suddenly remembering God's exhortation to combat pride with charity, I ordered a couple dozen pastries and brought them back to the office. When I arrived bearing that bright pink box, my coworkers were happy, and I felt good.

God, thank you for reminding me to look outside myself.

Pride goeth before destruction, and an haughty spirit before a fall.

–Proverbs 16:18

It used to be important to me to have the largest house on the block. It used to matter what type of car I drove. I took pride in my professional accomplishments, and I treated our possessions like personal trophies. I even began to pray less and stop reading the Bible as I focused on activities that would enrich my career and bring gains that are more material. Then, last year, we discovered that my wife is seriously ill. We were blindsided by the news; I had thought, on some level, that we were impervious to disaster. I thought my worldly success, which brought material riches, kept us safe. In these last months, as my wife has endured chemotherapy and bravely battled cancer, I have been humbled. I have also found solace in my faith.

God, too much pride in myself made me blind to what truly matters. Thank you for being there for me and those I love.

Let nothing be done through strife or vain-glory; but in lowliness of mind let each esteem other better than themselves.

–Philippians 2:3

I was proud when my middle-school-aged son participated in a local speech competition this spring. He placed well in the district levels, and will be moving on to compete at the county level. The county level, of course, will feature winners from other districts. All these kids will be "cream of the crop," which means that the competition will be stiffer. The event takes place next week, and my son is a little nervous about how well he will place. What if he does not get as high a ranking at the county level as he did at the district level? My wife and I have counseled him to just try hard, enjoy himself, and never lose sight of the difference between healthy competition and destructive rivalry.

Dear Lord, thank you for guiding my son and his peers to respect one another as they strive to do their best.

> *He that is void of wisdom despiseth his neighbour: but a man of understanding holdeth his peace.*
>
> –Proverbs 11:12

I am proud of my daughter. At 13, she is wise beyond her years. She is well liked by her teachers and peers, and a gifted musician. It's tempting, sometimes, to want to broadcast her accomplishments: the straight As she got on her last report card; the fact that she snagged a lead in the spring play. But I remember my mom used to shake her head when she'd encounter acquaintances who always seemed to go on and on about their own kids. She'd say to me privately, "Your dad and I are so proud of you kids, but our children speak for themselves by the way they are in the world." I was always struck by her grace, and the faith she had in us kids. Her example is an inspiration to me now that I am a parent myself.

Dear Lord, may I steer clear of bragging; rather may I celebrate the joy I take in my daughter with quiet grace.

And why beholdest thou the mote that is in thy brother's eye, but considerest not the beam that is in thine own eye?

–Matthew 7:3

Lord, my pride sometimes tempts me to judge others. From celebrity magazines to reality TV to social networking, it seems that very little in life is private anymore. This does not explain away some of the comments I find myself making, though. Throughout your Word you make it clear that your gift of salvation is available to everyone. Put this utmost in my mind when my pride tempts me to pass judgment on those around me.

Open rebuke is better than secret love. Faithful are the wounds of a friend; but the kisses of an enemy are deceitful.

–Proverbs 27:5-6

Father, it stings when the ones I love correct me. I don't like to be wrong or feel like I'm being criticized. But that's just wounded pride revealing itself. Deep down I appreciate learning the truth so I can learn and grow. Flattery feels nice in the moment, but it doesn't do much real good. People who risk hurting me because they love me are the ones I should listen to. Help me get over my wounded pride quickly and move on in light of what I've learned. And bless those who care enough for me to speak the truth in love.

I have therefore whereof I may glory through Jesus Christ in those things which pertain to God.

—Romans 15:17

Yesterday I took my son, Jason, and a few of his friends to pack food for a local religious organization that helps feed families in need. The kids were happy and excited. The warehouse where we worked had music playing, and our group felt good about the amount of work we got done. That night, as I tucked my son into bed, I told him that I was very proud of what he'd accomplished. "We did a good thing, didn't we?" he said. We talked about the kids who will benefit from the food; we talked about how doing good is one way to honor God. Then Jason asked if it was okay to be proud of the work we'd done that day. "Sometimes pride is bad, right?" he said. I agreed that sometimes it is. Sometimes pride can hobble us, or make us blind to things that are more important. "But it's totally okay to be proud of our works for God!" I assured him. "Helping makes me feel good," Jason agreed soberly. I hugged him, and felt so close to my boy.

God, thank you for the opportunity to do good in your name.

Wherefore I say unto thee, Her sins, which are many, are forgiven; for she loved much: but to whom little is forgiven, the same loveth little.

–Luke 7:47

Lord, it is tempting and easy to cast a scornful eye on those around us and note every fault. When my pride tempts me to do so, prompt me to turn the magnifying glass on myself instead. If I keep in mind how much I need your forgiveness every day, my love for you will never grow cold. I know you are willing to forgive each and every fault if I only ask.

> *But he giveth more grace. Wherefore he saith, God resisteth the proud, but giveth grace unto the humble.*
>
> –James 4:6

I do things I am proud of now and then, but I have to remember that any pride I have belongs to God. It humbles me when I realize that by myself I can do nothing, but with God all things become possible. My successes are his successes. My accomplishments are his accomplishments.

God, I pray you keep me humble enough to know who deserves the gratitude for all my blessings and miracles. Keep me wise enough to recognize your grace working in my life and not take credit for it myself. Pride limits me, but living in your will gives me unlimited access to the promises of the kingdom of heaven. May I remain always your humble servant, God.

A man's pride shall bring him low: but honour shall uphold the humble in spirit.

–Proverbs 29:23

Most of us realize that we are naturally self-centered, and we often respond to those around us in ways that make us appear proud, haughty, or arrogant. But if we look at Jesus' life, we see an excellent example of humility–an example that we should strive to follow. He taught that pride was destructive, but humility was powerful. Rather than touting his own greatness, Jesus was willing to kneel down and wash the feet of others, to show that we should all be servants to each other–and to God.

CHAPTER 7

STRESS AND WORRY

Cast thy burden upon the Lord, and he shall sustain thee: he shall never suffer the righteous to be moved.

–Psalm 55:22

I will lift up mine eyes unto the hills, from whence cometh my help. My help cometh from the Lord, which made heaven and earth.

–Psalm 121:1–2

Lord, you promise a helping hand in hard times. Today, I pray for all those who are in desperate need of help in order to survive: victims of earthquakes and tornadoes, the homeless, and the physically and emotionally destitute people of our world. Make yourself known to them, Lord. May they all see that their true help comes only from you! You who created them will not leave them without help, nor without hope.

> *Therefore I say unto you, Take no thought for your life, what ye shall eat, or what ye shall drink; nor yet for your body, what ye shall put on. Is not the life more than meat, and the body than raiment?*
>
> –Matthew 6:25

I recently graduated from college, and while I look for a job in my field of study, which is geology, I've been working a series of lower-paying jobs to pay the bills. I have managed to create a life I'm proud of: I pride myself on being independent, and don't live beyond my means. But my student loan debt is substantial, and there are not too many miles left on the old car I've been driving since high school. My current jobs do not offer health insurance. Some days I feel discouraged that I have not yet found the work for which my education has prepared me. Some nights I can't sleep for worrying about finances, or what expenses lie around the corner.

God, help me to remember that you are there: to support me, and imbue me with strength and wisdom. Help me to remember that you will provide.

Be careful for nothing; but in every thing by prayer and supplication with thanksgiving let your requests be made known unto God.

–Philippians 4:6

Lord, thank you for paying attention. Often I feel invisible, as if my problems are hidden from everyone. I long for someone to understand me, to recognize my situation, to see that I need a helping hand or a kind word. But I can rest in the knowledge that you see me. You know exactly what I'm up against and precisely what I need. You listen to my cries for help and hear every syllable of my prayers. And that's why I pray to you now. Lord, please take a good look at my circumstances and step in to help me. Encourage me, enliven me, and empower me through your grace. Amen.

God is our refuge and strength, a very present help in trouble.

–Psalm 46:1

I am the single father of two teens. The last year has been challenging for me as a parent: my daughter has had a hard time adjusting to the rigors of high school academics, and my son has been testing boundaries when it comes to curfews and expectations at home. Some nights I am troubled by insomnia, and then the next day, I have a shorter fuse. Tempers flare.

Dear Lord, please help me to remember that you are there for me. You are the answer to my anxiety. Help me to parent with wisdom and rely on you, even when I feel stressed and uncertain.

For with God nothing shall be impossible.

–Luke 1:37

I am enduring a dark period, God. Alzheimer's disease ravages my beloved father, and I must assist him and my mother while I try to raise my own three children with strength, patience, and joy. Some nights I lie awake, filled with fear that my little family will not survive this next chapter—one of many "Sandwich Generation" families with children and parents to care for.

Dear God, help me remain faithful to the promise that with you, nothing is impossible, even if I can't see through it for myself.

Take therefore no thought for the morrow: for the morrow shall take thought for the things of itself. Sufficient unto the day is the evil thereof.

–Matthew 6:34

It's easy to "borrow trouble," even on days when all seems well. This week was a good one: I met a challenging project deadline and received good feedback on the work I'd done. My daughter, who loves music, made it into a prestigious jazz band at school. Our crocuses started blooming, a sure sign that spring is here. And yet, as I poked around the garden, a place that always brings me solace, I found myself worrying about the day when my health might no longer allow me the pleasures I enjoy today. What if my knees give out, as they did for my father, and I could no longer kneel in my garden to plant and weed? What if someday I don't have the stamina to meet tight work deadlines as I do today? Then my daughter came racing outside to join me. She wanted to talk about how to sensitively share news of her acceptance to the jazz band with another friend who did not make the cut. We talked, and our conversation was real and good. My wife poked her head out the door, informing us that she was making a special dinner to celebrate the successful completion of my work project. I let myself be in that moment, and in that moment, I felt joy.

God, please help me to stay in the here and now, with its joys and puzzles–not waste my strength on worry about what might happen tomorrow, or in all the days to come.

They that sow in tears shall reap in joy.

—Psalm 126:5

I'm an emergency room nurse and love my job, which can be by turns intense, interesting, and challenging. No two days are alike, though much of the time I am invited to think on my feet. I do like that aspect of the job. But lately, the ER has been so busy that by shift's end I find myself exhausted, both mentally and physically. I must remember that what I do has value, and these things run in cycles. I've worked long enough to understand that the pace will eventually settle, at least temporarily, and that I mustn't let a hard day of work get me down.

Dear God, help me to take the long view. Remind me, on the days when my spirits and energy are low, that ultimately things always get better.

Behold, I will bring it health and cure, and I will cure them, and will reveal unto them the abundance of peace and truth.

–Jeremiah 33:6

Mental illness can be so devastating and stigmatizing, Lord. Few understand the heartaches involved in diseases that carry no apparent physical scars. Be with those friends, neighbors, and family members who deal daily with difficult situations of which we are often unaware. Touch them with your special love, and let them know that they can lean on you, Lord. Ease their burdens, quell their sadness, and calm their desperation. Bring peace and healing to these households. Remind them of the promise of your everlasting love.

Yea, though I walk through the valley of the shadow of death, I will fear no evil: for thou art with me; thy rod and thy staff they comfort me.

–Psalm 23:4

This past year has been a challenging one. My son Jeff, who began his freshman year at university in the fall, became overwhelmed by his course work: his physical and emotional health suffered. After flunking several of his first-semester classes, he recently returned home. My wife and I are doing our best to support him emotionally, and we have talked, as a family, about Jeff getting a job and earning some extra money while he regroups. We've also talked about him taking some classes at the local community college. But he is very depressed and finding it difficult to make decisions, and I myself am deeply saddened by his unhappiness and confusion.

Dear Lord, your loving presence provides solace. Please comfort Jeff. Please fill my heart, and help my wife and me to know how to encourage our son and help him work through this difficult chapter.

Heaviness in the heart of man maketh it stoop: but a good word maketh it glad.

—Proverbs 12:25

We never know what's going on in the life of another person. The guy who cuts me off in traffic, the checkout clerk who reacts to a query with impatience: the way someone reacts doesn't always reflect how they feel about me; it is often instead a response to the complex circumstances of their life on that given day.

God, help me remember to respond to others with grace and kindness—to put good out into the world just for the sake of doing so—for the right words spoken to someone at the right time might lift the worry that burdens another's heart.

Search me, O God, and know my heart: try me, and know my thoughts.

–Psalm 139:23

It is not always easy to understand others; it is not always easy to understand oneself! This came home to me last week, when I "woke up on the wrong side of the bed." From the moment I got up to make coffee, I was filled with a pervasive sense of anxiety. I tried to take care, giving myself extra time for my commute to work, and organizing my day to minimize stress. And yet nothing seemed to help until I had the sense to close my office door, put my phone aside, and say the quiet, simple prayer, "Help." I won't tell you that my anxiety magically went away, for it did not. But I had a moment to collect myself, to register some of the things that had piled up throughout the week–a bad grade my son earned in math, the leaky faucet, the fact that I haven't been sleeping as well–and the understanding gave me some context, and consequently some relief. Understanding our own concerns is a part of our ongoing education as to who we are as people.

God, you have the power to look into my mind and soul to know what causes my anxiety. Thank you for helping me to remember that. Thank you for being there to guide me.

Peace I leave with you, my peace I give unto you: not as the world giveth, give I unto you. Let not your heart be troubled, neither let it be afraid.

–John 14:27

O Lord God, who has given us the night for rest, I pray that in my sleep my soul may remain awake to you, steadfastly adhering to your love. As I lay aside my cares to relax and relieve my mind, may I not forget your infinite and unresting care for me. And in this way, let my conscience be at peace, so that when I rise tomorrow, I am refreshed in body, mind and soul.

–John Calvin

Casting all your care upon him; for he careth for you.

–1 Peter 5:7

At work, I manage a team of employees, and it's part of my job to take charge and support those who report to me. Questions? Come to me. Problems? I can help solve them. I take pride in this role, and yet there are times in my own life when I need to remember that I don't have to handle everything. I can–and should–take my problems to God. He actually encourages us to do so because he loves us.

Dear Lord, please help me to remember that I can rely on you.

God, hear my prayer. Bless me with patience and a steadfast heart to help me get through such emotionally trying times. Heal the wounds of my heart and soul with the soothing balm of your comforting presence, that I may be able to love and to live again. Amen.

It's amazing, steadfast God, how much better I feel after sharing with you even the smallest doubt or little niggling worry about being the best I can be. Connected, we can do great things. Alone, I am the victim of my own fears.

Last weekend, I was busy washing the car, cutting the grass, and taking my good shirts to the dry cleaners. My daughter asked if I might take a break and read with her, and I responded that I had a mile-long list of things to do and no time in which to do them. "We have nice things and I like to keep them nice!" I replied. I felt stressed after we talked, but managed to congratulate myself. After all, I was giving my daughter a good lesson in responsibility and the importance of taking care of our possessions. I even felt proud of how good the car looked as I drove to the cleaners, and started planning what projects in the house I'd tackle upon returning home. But as I drove, it occurred to me: was having a perfectly clean car as important as time with my child? In ten years, when she's gone to college, will it matter that my home was always spotless? I took a breath and retrenched: there were definitely things I needed to accomplish that day, but I understood, suddenly, that time with my kid was important, too—some things could wait.

My daughter and I ended up walking to the library when I returned home. We not only read together there, but we had a good, easy conversation that emerged naturally as we walked. I learned some things about her school week that I doubt she'd have shared if we hadn't had some quality time. House projects? If anything, what I probably need to focus on is streamlining my belongings!

God, help me to remember that having too many things can be a source of worry. The more I own, the more I worry about protecting or maintaining. Life is more than material possessions.

CHAPTER 8

MARRIAGE

Husbands, love your wives, even as Christ also loved the church, and gave himself for it.

–Ephesians 5:25

Awake, O north wind; and come, thou south; blow upon my garden, that the spices thereof may flow out. Let my beloved come into his garden, and eat his pleasant fruits.

–Song of Solomon 4:16

Marriage, Lord, is like a garden: You don't keep digging up a plant to see if its roots are growing! Sustain us, for there are seasons of wilted growth just as there are seasons of blossom and fruit. While ripening to become useful, may we love one another with the same strengthening trust and patience you, gardener of the world, show toward us.

And blessed is she that believed: for there shall be a performance of those things which were told her from the Lord.

–Luke 1:45

Our relationships strengthen us. This came home to me the other day, when an exchange with a coworker left me feeling irresolute and unsettled. During my commute home, my stomach was in knots: I went over and over the disagreement in my head. It was hard to sort out whether I'd handled things with grace. When I got home, I found that my wife had started dinner; the warm atmosphere of love and regard unclenched my heart, and I was able to talk frankly about the day. My wife's nonjudgmental but clear-sighted perspective helped me sort how to remedy the situation; after we talked, we took a moment to pray together.

God, thank you for reminding us of the importance of believing: in you, and in one another.

And if one prevail against him, two shall withstand him; and a threefold cord is not quickly broken.

–Ecclesiastes 4:12

My wife and I don't attend church every Sunday, but each weekend we make time to read scripture and talk about the week, which we try to view through the lens of spirituality. A difficult coworker, good news in our extended families–we'll discuss the good and the bad and talk about how God informs each ebb and flow. Sometimes we'll share a joy, such as the time my wife built a new bird feeder and we both discovered the great calm and pleasure we derived from watching the sparrows and finches. I think we both gain a lot from these quiet, regular moments of sharing. The Bible reminds me how your presence in my life, and my wife's life, creates a powerful "threefold cord."

God, if my marriage is grounded in you, it will be strong.

> *What therefore God hath joined together, let not man put asunder.*
>
> –Mark 10:9

My wife and I have encountered a rough patch in our marriage. Our youngest child recently began college, and transitioning to an "empty nest" home has been harder on us both than we anticipated. My wife, who misses our sons, has started a new job. She's not home as much just as I've begun contemplating taking early retirement. So many days we seem to be at cross-purposes—we seem to want different things! But this morning when we sat down together over coffee, my wife reminded me that over the years, we have weathered many storms in our marriage—job loss, the deaths of our parents, our middle son's struggles with schoolwork and drugs. Each time we have prevailed together. It was a good conversation, and I think we felt closer to one another than we have in months.

Dear Lord, you have joined my wife and me. You have blessed our partnership. To succeed, we must take the long view!

With all lowliness and meekness, with long-suffering, forbearing one another in love; Endeavouring to keep the unity of the Spirit in the bond of peace.

–Ephesians 4:2–3

One of many things I like about my wife is her ability to laugh at herself. She doesn't take herself too seriously, and because I admire that quality in her, and know that I myself can tend to pride, I try as best I can to emulate her humility. Just yesterday, we were talking about my efforts to fix the sink in the bathroom, and when I caught myself becoming defensive (even, I have to admit, a little self-important), I tried to turn things around by joking. I think my wife was probably relieved to see me making an effort, and so she took up with the joke. Within moments we were both laughing. Things could have gone one way but they took a better turn.

Dear Lord, thank you for helping me to remember the importance of humility in a marriage.

> *And above all things have fervent charity among yourselves: for charity shall cover the multitude of sins.*
>
> –1 Peter 4:8

My wife and I are newly married, and we have encountered some growing pains as we adjust to sharing a home and making a life together. One persistent source of discord is the fact that I am something of a neatnik, while my wife is more relaxed about keeping our apartment tidy. I can see that she tries, but it still drives me a little crazy when she leaves dirty dishes on the counter, or toothpaste spatters in the sink. These are such little things, but sometimes they get to me, and I said as much to my father the last time we were together. Dad has been married to my mom for more than 30 years, and he responded to me with gentle humor: "Choose your battles, son, and remember: love helps us overlook one another's flaws." My parents have an extraordinarily loving marriage, and Dad's words have stayed with me.

Dear Lord, please help me remember that love is the root of a strong marriage, and that love helps us accept our partners as they are, warts and all.

Bless this gathering of what, at first glance, looks like mismatched parts, encircling God, for we want to become a family. Guide us as we step closer to one another, but not so close as to crowd. Heal wounds from past events that made this union possible.

Bless the children with the courage to try new relatives, new traditions, new homes. Empower them in their anger, helping them know that it is okay and that tears are healing. Assure them that they have the strength to live in two worlds and hearts big enough to love others. Make us, the step-adults, worthy of this love, for it comes at great cost. Help us respect previous traditions and loves and not step too close in our need to belong. For even in the midst of celebrating, there is mourning.

Remind us to take baby steps as we become all you have in mind. Your presence will be our companion, your love our protection, and your wisdom our guidance in this awesome responsibility. Step closer, loving God, and lead us.

And the Lord God said, It is not good that the man should be alone; I will make him an help meet for him.

–Genesis 2:18

My wife and I have been married for 25 years. Around the time we celebrated that milestone anniversary, we each began to pursue self-employment ventures that allow us to work from home. Several friends have laughingly asked if we get on one another's nerves, but working from home has actually been a real joy for us both. We like working together in the living room with music playing in the background. We both love the company of our cats. I really enjoy that my wife and I can eat lunch together, and sometimes we'll take a break in the afternoon and swim laps at the Y. My wife is my best friend.

God, thank you for the everyday companionship that a strong marriage brings.

Therefore shall a man leave his father and his mother, and shall cleave unto his wife: and they shall be one flesh.

–Genesis 2:24

Lord, we lift up our marriage to you with thanks for the gift you gave us when you first brought us together: it isn't as fresh and new as it was when you created it for us, Lord, so we ask your blessing again. Wrap the life we share in your protective arms so that the world will never be able to tear us apart. Fill us anew with the precious love you gave us for one another. Hold us firmly in your eternal love. Amen.

Whoso findeth a wife findeth a good thing, and obtaineth favour of the Lord.

—Proverbs 18:22

There is no greater mystery than love, Lord of covenants and promises. We are in its presence on this anniversary day. Bless those who live, day after day after ordinary day, within the fullness of married love, surely one of life's greatest mysteries. Bless them as they honor their past, even while they create a future. Let them bask in the pleasures and applause of today, when we bow before their accomplishments, which, like the rings we read on the inner souls of trees, are an inspiration and blessing to us all.

And be ye kind one to another, tenderhearted, forgiving one another, even as God for Christ's sake hath forgiven you.

–Ephesians 4:32

Almighty God, I honestly don't know how a marriage survives without forgiveness. In fact, maybe the marriages without it don't survive. Thank you for a forgiving wife, Lord. Because she forgives me so often, it's much easier for me to forgive her when she does something thoughtless. Forgiveness prevents the weeds from taking root in a relationship and provides an environment where love can grow. Bless our marriage, Lord, and keep it well watered with forgiveness.

CHAPTER 9
WISDOM

There is no wisdom nor understanding nor counsel against the Lord.

—Proverbs 21:30

The heart of the prudent getteth knowledge; and the ear of the wise seeketh knowledge.

–Proverbs 18:15

My wife and I had our first and only child, Amanda, later in life, and honestly, that child has been a gift in ways I never could have anticipated. One way our daughter has enriched my life is that, truly, she keeps me learning and growing. Amanda has such diverse interests. Through her, I've been introduced to anime movies, and new styles of music. She has even gotten me interested in the works of Edgar Allan Poe! These are areas I had never explored previously, and I appreciate being able to experience them with my child.

Thank you, God, for the gift of a child who reminds me to never stop learning. May I always be a student of life.

With the ancient is wisdom; and in length of days understanding. With him is wisdom and strength, he hath counsel and understanding.

–Job 12:12–13

My parents died when I was a young man, barely out of school, and at first, I proceeded through life almost blindly. I made my way as best I could, but sometimes it was a lonely road. I have learned in the years since that God puts people into my path, to help guide me, and when I remain open, I can benefit from the knowledge others have to share. Many of these folks are older than me. They possess the wisdom born of experience, and a broad worldview that helps me to keep perspective.

Dear Lord, please may I always remember to seek instruction from those who have gone down the path before me.

He that hath knowledge spareth his words: and a man of understanding is of an excellent spirit.

—Proverbs 17:27

When I was a young man, I felt invincible. I didn't think there was anything anyone else could teach me. Like many young men before me, I delighted in pontificating and boasting to anyone who might be within hearing. In retrospect, I see that I mistook saying something for actually having something to say! At my first real job, I came under the supervision of a quiet, much older man. He was clearly respected by his peers, and yet he spoke little. During meetings, he'd listen quietly. When he did speak, everyone paid attention. As time went on, I began to want to emulate his style, and so I asked him about it. "Don't talk until you really have something to say," he counseled. "And by listening, you'll learn a lot in the meantime." His words have stayed with me.

God, please always help me remember that to learn, I am wise to speak less and listen more.

If any of you lack wisdom, let him ask of God, that giveth to all men liberally, and upbraideth not; and it shall be given him.

—James 1:5

I recently took on a new position at work. It's a stretch for me, and while I welcome the change (my previous duties no longer challenged me), I am also fearful of failure. My new position will require a steep learning curve, and demands that I oversee a number of employees. What if I can't master the material? What if I don't have what it takes to manage others wisely? But I must remember that God is always there to help me. He can increase wisdom—not just spiritually, but in all ways.

Dear Lord, please be with me as I challenge myself to develop intellectually and master new skills. Please help me to stay sharp, and to grow as a person, with energy and grace.

Even a fool, when he holdeth his peace, is counted wise: and he that shutteth his lips is esteemed a man of understanding.

—Proverbs 17:28

There is a time for speaking up, and a time for shutting up. Grant me the wisdom to always know the difference. My wife and kids say I talk too much, and I admit it has gotten me into hot water more than a few times, especially in arguments with family and people I work with. It is hard to stay quiet when someone presses your buttons and you want to react and respond, but it usually makes things worse. I ask, Lord, that you give me the wisdom to know when it is best to talk about a problem and offer a solution, and when to hang back and stay silent, not sticking my nose, or my voice, in other people's business.

Is this grace given . . . that now unto the principalities and powers in heavenly places might be known by the church the manifold wisdom of God.

–Ephesians 3:8, 10

God reveals his wisdom through his church. Somewhere in your neighborhood there is a group of imperfect people meeting together, seeking to know God and understand his word. And he promises to use them to encourage each other in this desire.

The Apostle Paul refers to "the fellowship of the mystery" (verse 9). God builds this fellowship, using the church to proclaim the gospel. The church is his body (Ephesians 1:22–23) and it is his bride (Ephesians 5:31–33). What tender images to describe communities of faith. And what a wonderful promise, that his wisdom is made known by the church.

The way of a fool is right in his own eyes: but he that hearkeneth unto counsel is wise.

—Proverbs 12:15

I am what they call a "self-made man." Right out of college, I started a little company with friends, and in only a few years, the enterprise has grown successful. My position requires that I manage a team of employees. My strategy has traditionally been a "tough love" approach. Not long ago, I was visiting my parents and my dad heard my interactions with an employee over the phone. Later that evening, he brought up the phone call and counseled me to soften my approach. "You've got to keep a light touch," he advised, and I immediately felt defensive. My business was doing well! It was my job to keep the others in line! And yet upon reflection, I remembered that my dad has a lifetime of experience to draw upon. Over the years, he has been respected—even loved—by those who report to him. Though I didn't want to hear it at the time, maybe he does have something to share.

Dear Lord, help me to remember that wisdom comes from listening to others.

> *Wisdom is the principal thing; therefore get wisdom: and with all thy getting get understanding.*
>
> —Proverbs 4:7

Not a day goes by when I don't do something without thinking, and regret it instantly. But I am trying, Lord. With all the distractions of life, I often act without first checking in with you and asking to discern your will and your wisdom. And, boy, do I pay the price for my ignorance and impatience when my problems get bigger, not smaller. But I am learning, Lord, and with each passing day I am stopping more often to ask for your wisdom for whatever situation or challenge I may be facing. I've found that wisdom trumps quick kneejerk reactions every time.

Thank you, Lord, for helping me to understand it's better to slow down, do the right thing, and avoid regrets about it later.

And God gave Solomon wisdom and understanding exceeding much, and largeness of heart, even as the sand that is on the sea shore.

–1 Kings 4:29

I don't have a lot of money, God, so when I think about giving to others, I often feel as though I have nothing of value to offer. Then I remember the times I sat with my grandparents before they passed away, listening to their stories and experiences, absorbing their wisdom, and cherishing their advice. I realized I have so much to offer to those around me. I have love and life experience and enough wisdom to help those who ask for it. I have a heart full of compassion and understanding. I have kindness. Thank you, God, for the gifts you instilled in me so I could pass them on to others . . . gifts no amount of money can buy.

Every word of God is pure: he is a shield unto them that put their trust in him.

—Proverbs 30:5

I have a friend who has read the Bible from cover to cover, and he described it as a profound experience. I have not read the Bible in this manner; I have favorite verses but, truth be told, the biblical prose can be intimidating. I do not always understand how the verses apply to my broken dishwasher or sick pet. And there are so many interpretations, sometimes conflicting, of what is within the Bible's pages!

God, grant me a clear, level head and an open heart so that I might understand the wise ways of your Word. May the rich stories, the adventures and drama, and instruction that the Bible has to offer, be accessible to me. May I have the wisdom to apply its contents to my day-to-day life, and may I always be open to your teachings.

And he changeth the times and the seasons: he removeth kings, and setteth up kings: he giveth wisdom unto the wise, and knowledge to them that know understanding.

–Daniel 2:21

Lord, sometimes I feel you've blessed me with all kinds of knowledge that no one is interested in hearing! Help me know when and how to share your wisdom with others. Help me to show others your truth, rather than just talk about it. You taught us by living out the truth, Lord. Help us to do the same.

CHAPTER 10
SERVING OTHERS

My little children, let us not love in word, neither in tongue; but in deed and in truth.

–1 John 3:18

And let us not be weary in well doing: for in due season we shall reap, if we faint not.

—Galatians 6:9

Henry's sister Ellie has suffered from depression for years. She's on medication now, which helps. And Henry tries to uplift her (and sometimes succeeds) with daily texts, movie nights together, and the occasional dinner out. "Ellie's depression has been a learning experience for me," Henry shares. "I can be there for her, I can't stop trying, but I cannot expect that every one of my efforts will make a difference. I have to be at peace with that."

Lord, I am discouraged because my efforts to serve others seem to mean little. Help me to not lose heart. Help me to keep trying.

So after he had washed their feet, and had taken his garments, and was set down again, he said unto them, Know ye what I have done to you? Ye call me Master and Lord: and ye say well; for so I am. If I then, your Lord and Master, have washed your feet; ye also ought to wash one another's feet.

–John 13:12–14

As a father of two little girls, I am deeply aware of how my children learn—not just from what I say, but what I do. Jesus set the example of service, and I try to set a good example of service for my children's sake. Every week, I take the kids to volunteer at a local animal shelter. I think it's good for my daughters to see their dad cheerfully and voluntarily offering time and effort to a cause he believes in, and it's something the three of us share every week. "It feels good to do something good, doesn't it?" my daughter said the other day. I feel happy for her that she's coming to that realization at a relatively young age.

God, thank you for my children. Thank you for helping me to teach them to put good out into the world.

As every man hath received the gift, even so minister the same one to another, as good stewards of the manifold grace of God.

—1 Peter 4:10

It is easier to serve others when my own life is going well. During those chapters in life when things are more or less on an even keel, I am filled with cheer, and I go out into the world wanting to share that goodwill. The act of service comes less easily to me when life presents challenges. When burdened by stress at work, say, or the struggles my son periodically faces from bullies at school, my tendency is to look inward.

God, teach me to strive to help others no matter what is going on in my life. You serve us regardless of externals. Service is a gift from you! Remembering this puts me in the right frame of mind to serve others.

For, brethren, ye have been called unto liberty; only use not liberty for an occasion to the flesh, but by love serve one another. For all the law is fulfilled in one word, even in this; Thou shalt love thy neighbour as thyself.

—Galatians 5:13–14

I am grateful to live in a democratic society where I can live freely and do as I please. I have a steady job, which consequently allows me to pursue multiple interests that include travel and food. I thoroughly enjoy exploring new cuisines, for example, and cooking for and eating out with friends. I feel lucky to be free to engage in such rewarding experiences—they "fill me up"—yet I also know that reaching out to others is an important part of becoming a fulfilled, evolved person. To that end, I recently signed up to volunteer with Meals on Wheels. I have already met some cool seniors, folks I likely would never have encountered in my usual orbit. I find myself looking forward to my interactions with them each week.

God, help me to honor the freedom I enjoy by helping others, not just by indulging myself.

If we are devoted to the cause of humanity, we shall soon be crushed and broken-hearted...but if our motive is love to God, no ingratitude can hinder us from serving our fellow men.

–Oswald Chambers

Lord, today I ask you to slow me down and open my ears so I will notice the needs of those around me. Too often I breeze by people with an offhand greeting but remain in a cocoon of my own concerns. I know many around me are hurting, Lord. Help me find ways to be of service.

I have shewed you all things, how that so labouring ye ought to support the weak, and to remember the words of the Lord Jesus, how he said, It is more blessed to give than to receive.

–Acts 20:35

I am grateful for the blessings in my life: a strong marriage, good health, and a steady job. I firmly believe that these advantages put me in a position to help those less fortunate than myself. On a fundamental level, I think that's why we're here–to assist others. But some days I do grow weary of the work constant service (either service I've elected to do or that has been thrust upon me) requires. On those days, God, please help me to remember how giving fills one spiritually. Christ taught that it is better to give than to receive; please help me to remember this on the days that I struggle.

> *With good will doing service, as to the Lord, and not to men.*
>
> —Ephesians 6:7

When Joey's friend Matt was struggling through a divorce, Joey tried to be present for his friend, offering rides, hot meals, and a listening ear. Matt, consumed with anxiety about his future, was not always appreciative of the sacrifices Joey made to support him. "It was a tough year," Joey remembers now. "Our friendship has regained its balance, but there were times I prayed for guidance because I felt Matt was taking my efforts for granted."

Dear God, my efforts to serve others are not always reciprocated—or even appreciated. May I do the right thing for you, not for gratitude or anything I might receive in return.

Then said Jesus unto his disciples, If any man will come after me, let him deny himself, and take up his cross, and follow me. For whosoever will save his life shall lose it: and whosoever will lose his life for my sake shall find it.

–Matthew 16:24–25

A few days after retiring, Virgil visited the local hospital and asked how he could be of service. His kids were grown, and he and his wife had divorced a decade ago. He wanted to define a new way to make a difference. "My volunteer work fulfills me," Virgil says now. "I feel I am manifesting Christ's teachings when I help others; serving God in this way helps me realize my best self."

Dear Lord, may I always remember that self-realization is achieved through my service to you.

Therefore all things whatsoever ye would that men should do to you, do ye even so to them.

–Matthew 7:12

Lord, my father was a spiritual man, not always because of what he said but because of his actions. Everything he did, whether he was making bookshelves or helping us with our math, he did with love and mindfulness. Dad's life of quiet service was a direct application of Christ's teachings. He never called attention to the caring things he did. My father died last year and I miss him every day.

God, please help me to carry on what Dad personified; help me to remember that saying words of glory and praise is not the same thing as doing your will.

The first of all the commandments is, Hear, O Israel; The Lord our God is one Lord: And thou shalt love the Lord thy God with all thy heart, and with all thy soul, and with all thy mind, and with all thy strength: this is the first commandment. And the second is like, namely this, Thou shalt love thy neighbour as thyself. There is none other commandment greater than these.

–Mark 12:29-31

One of the principle rules of religion is to lose no occasion of serving God. And since he is invisible to our eyes, we are to serve him in our neighbor, which he receives as if done to himself in person, standing visibly before us.

–John Wesley

But exhort one another daily, while it is called To day; lest any of you be hardened through the deceitfulness of sin.

—Hebrews 3:13

Rob loves his brother Jim; he also knows Jim struggles with a gambling addiction. The brothers were driving together to a wedding, and their travels took them past a casino. Jim wanted to stop. Rob didn't want conflict, but he stood firm. "It was hard for me to confront him, but we actually had a good talk," Rob says now. "And we didn't go to the casino. That day, Jim needed me to help him do the right thing."

Dear God, please be with me. When I see someone tempted or vulnerable, help me to reach out and offer encouragement.

Blessed be God, even the Father of our Lord Jesus Christ, the Father of mercies, and the God of all comfort; Who comforteth us in all our tribulation, that we may be able to comfort them which are in any trouble, by the comfort wherewith we ourselves are comforted of God.

–2 Corinthians 1:3–4

Lord, today I ask you to bless and comfort all who daily see pain and desperation as part of their jobs. Bless the social workers, Lord, and comfort them with the knowledge that what they do truly matters. Bless the doctors and nurses working with the seriously ill, and comfort them with your insight. Bless and comfort the caretakers toiling through the night, Lord, and send your strength to restore them. All these people are serving you as they serve others. Please give them your special blessing. Amen.

Open thy mouth, judge righteously, and plead the cause of the poor and needy.

—Proverbs 31:9

When Ryan's friend Nora encouraged him to join in a neighborhood effort to go door to door and collect canned goods for the homeless, Ryan was at first hesitant; his natural shyness seemed to preclude such activity. But after praying and reflecting on his fears, Ryan decided to move outside his comfort zone and help out. The experience was uplifting: it felt good to be acting—and speaking—on behalf of those in need.

Lord, please embolden me to speak out for those less fortunate than myself.

CHAPTER 11
MATERIALISM AND WEALTH

He that trusteth in his riches shall fall; but the righteous shall flourish as a branch.

–Proverbs 11:28

But if any provide not for his own, and specially for those of his own house, he hath denied the faith, and is worse than an infidel.

—1 Timothy 5:8

When my stepfather died, he left a sum of money to me. I was surprised and at first a little overwhelmed, but after a brief period of what I can only call dazed euphoria, my wife and I consulted with a financial planner. We wanted to be wise stewards of this unexpected income. After our meeting with the advisor, we determined that we would use a large portion of the money for our daughter's college education, and then put aside the rest for retirement. Because of health concerns I've been facing, it is important to me to know that my wife will have money to draw upon in the likely event that I die before she does.

God, wealth gives me an obligation to provide for my family. I am grateful for the means to do so.

Lay not up for yourselves treasures upon earth, where moth and rust doth corrupt, and where thieves break through and steal: But lay up for yourselves treasures in heaven, where neither moth nor rust doth corrupt, and where thieves do not break through nor steal: For where your treasure is, there will your heart be also.

—Matthew 6:19–21

When my wife and I were first married, we were what I think is sometimes called "house proud": we would spend weeks looking for just the right couch; even a dish drainer was chosen after great deliberation. We put a lot of energy into making our home look a certain way, and we took pride in our possessions. Then my wife got pregnant. When our daughter was born, the "look" of the house was sometimes sacrificed for the practicalities of baby accouterments. As our daughter grew, we adopted two cats. That couch we chose with such care has taken quite a beating. With kids and pets running around, the house isn't quite the showplace we nurtured 10 years ago. But it's a happy home, filled with artwork and books and love. Sometimes things break. Sometimes things get torn or stained. It doesn't seem to matter the way it once did.

Thank you, God, for helping me to learn where my treasure truly lies.

And he said unto them, Take heed, and beware of covetousness: for a man's life consisteth not in the abundance of the things which he possesseth.

–Luke 12:15

My wife and I attended a party the other night, and the subject of real estate came up. I love our modest home. We raised our kids there, and we've always been comfortable. But when conversation turned to what makes a house "sell-able," I became embarrassed. We don't have granite countertops in our kitchen, and the bathrooms, while bright, have outdated fixtures. I came home feeling jealous and uneasy: a spirit of materialism briefly made me see our cozy home in a less flattering light. When I woke the next morning, though, refreshed by sleep, my wife and I enjoyed our coffee while watching the birds from our breakfast nook. I looked around our little house and felt joy.

God, you have graced our home with your love. May I not allow materialism to distract me or create anxiety; may I be grateful for the true blessings in my life.

Denying ungodliness and worldly lusts, we should live soberly, righteously, and godly, in this present world.

–Titus 2:12

Have you ever met someone who solely defines themselves by their possessions? Though society may seem to reward those who achieve their self-worth from having the "right" car, or the biggest house, these individuals are, at the root of it, unhappy people. Material gain in and of itself is, ultimately, an empty victory. Don't be that person. Don't let your worldly interests cloud your true sense of self.

Dear God, may what really matters define who I am as a person!

Let your conversation be without covetousness; and be content with such things as ye have: for he hath said, I will never leave thee, nor forsake thee.

—Hebrews 13:5

My wife has become friendly with some of the other parents at our son's school, and we were recently invited to a barbecue hosted by one of her new acquaintances. When we arrived the night of the event, I saw that the house was a very large, modern house, probably worth three times the price of our modest ranch-style home. I felt a twinge of envy, only exacerbated when the host, a cheerful, bluff man, invited me downstairs to see the movie theater he'd had built, and a custom wine cellar. I got through the evening by smiling mechanically. I could only imagine what my wife was thinking. Did she wish we lived in this type of house? Did she envy the host's wife, who had a state-of-the-art kitchen? Later that night, as we wound down before bed, my wife noted, "They are really nice people. But gosh, that house is so big! It seemed a little impersonal, you know? I prefer our messy little house; it seems like home!"

Dear God, protect me from envying what others have, when my own life is so rich!

But godliness with contentment is great gain. For we brought nothing into this world, and it is certain we can carry nothing out. And having food and raiment let us be therewith content.

–1 Timothy 6:6–8

Content with just food and clothing? Really, Lord? I'm thankful that you provide for my basic needs, but there's much, much more on my wish list. This passage makes me realize how much I expect in life. Sometimes I act like I'm entitled to certain things: a well-paying job for little effort on my part, minimal traffic on the way to said job, restaurant lunches every day, seamless relationships with loved ones. Help me to be thankful for the countless blessings in my life and to always be ready to help others rather than focusing on adding to my own stores. Please guide me, Lord. I'm ready to answer your call to contentment.

For all that is in the world, the lust of the flesh, and the lust of the eyes, and the pride of life, is not of the Father, but is of the world.

–1 John 2:16

I recently had lunch with an old college friend, Doug, who always lifts my spirits when we get together. I was excited to share that we've recently purchased a new car. With my youngest daughter out of college, we enjoy a little more disposable income, and so my wife and I splurged on a vehicle loaded with extras. I could tell my friend was happy for me, but as I returned to the car in conversation again and again, I noticed Doug's eyes starting to glaze over. That gave me pause, and I had enough sense to switch gears. I asked about the mission work Doug will be doing in the coming year. Doug, in turn, asked about my daughter's graduation, and our lunch got back on track. I parted from my friend feeling restored, and thankful I'd caught myself before our time together was soured by too much focus on possessions.

Lord, thank you for reminding me that it's okay to enjoy material things, but they are just that—things. Being fixated on belongings is not from God.

Turn ye not unto idols, nor make to yourselves molten gods: I am the Lord your God.

–Leviticus 19:4

Lord, if only all the false gods that lure us were clearly labeled. We are introduced to worldly ambition, wealth, physical perfection, romance–any number of attractive enticements–and it isn't until we realize that the pursuit of them is using up way too much of our resources that we discover we have made these things our gods. Forgive us, Lord. Help us to keep even good things in balance and never to pursue anything with more fervor than we pursue our relationship with you.

He that loveth silver shall not be satisfied with silver; nor he that loveth abundance with increase: this is also vanity.

–Ecclesiastes 5:10

For a period of years, I enjoyed a high-powered job with a significant income. I enjoyed the perks money can buy–a nice house, a good car, and designer clothing. But looking back, I can see that I labored under the misconception that possessions would bring me lasting satisfaction. Unfortunately, that was not the case. Soon after I bought and furnished my home, it occurred to me how nice it would be to have a second home. I loved my car until a colleague got a newer, improved model. I spent a lot of time just maintaining my possessions–taking the car in to be washed and detailed, hiring people to keep the houses clean–and many days, I felt dissatisfied. It was only when I made the decision to simplify my life, to divest myself of some of the possessions that were taking up so much of my time and focus instead on matters of substance, including my relationships with others and my own spirituality, that I gained some measure of peace. The problem with money and acquisition is there is no end–no level of satisfaction.

God, help me to stay focused on what really matters.

Now therefore fear ye not: I will nourish you, and your little ones. And he comforted them, and spake kindly unto them.

–Genesis 50:21

Money is a big issue for most people. Either we don't have enough, or we worry about losing what we have. We are afraid of being left homeless and destitute. But God promises he will comfort and nourish us, with material things and things no amount of money can buy. God tells us not to be afraid.

Dear God, I pray to worry less, and have more faith in your promise of prosperity. Even when my wallet looks empty, I know that blessings are happening in the unseen and will soon be made manifest. You never fail to sustain and support me, God. I pray for your care and comfort in good financial times and in bad.

But seek ye first the kingdom of God, and his righteousness; and all these things shall be added unto you.

–Matthew 6:33

There is no denying the pleasure of creature comforts. Last year, my wife and I decided to take the plunge and have central air conditioning installed in our old home. Every hot day this summer, I have reveled in returning to a blast of cool air when I get home; on some level, the air conditioning has made my life better. But as much as I appreciate it, I must remember not to be distracted by or consumed by physical comforts to the extent that I neglect my spiritual welfare.

Dear God, thank you for air conditioning--it is good to feel good! But may I always be cognizant of well-being on the inside as well as the outside; may my focus on the everlasting rewards of your kingdom be unswerving.

CHAPTER 12
RELATIONSHIPS

A new commandment I give unto you, That ye love one another; as I have loved you, that ye also love one another.

–John 13:34

And as ye would that men should do to you, do ye also to them likewise.

—Luke 6:31

Yesterday I got into a car accident. It was my fault—I was in a hurry and tried to cross an intersection just as yellow turned to red—but I felt defensive and berated the driver whose car I had clipped. I was embarrassed when the driver met my bluster with calm grace; later, after I'd regained my composure, it also struck me how much I appreciated being spoken to respectfully, though I myself had been less than gracious. The other driver's consideration made an impression, and when I told my wife about it, she smiled gently and observed, "That guy was probably just treating you the way he wished you'd treat him!"

God, remind me to treat others as I would want them to treat me.

And it came to pass, when he had made an end of speaking unto Saul, that the soul of Jonathan was knit with the soul of David, and Jonathan loved him as his own soul.

–1 Samuel 18:1

Ethan was nervous about starting college, and when he met his new roommate, he was filled with trepidation. A bookish, shy boy, Ethan felt intimidated by Kyle, an artist with dyed blue hair who carried himself with confidence. In fact, the two became fast friends, despite–or maybe because of–their differences. "I'm a more well-rounded person, thanks to my friendship with Kyle," Ethan says now. "And I think he'd say the same."

Dear God, David was an enemy of Saul–and yet Saul's own son Jonathan became David's close friend. Please help me to remember that you can unite even unlikely people in friendship.

Fret not thyself because of evildoers, neither be thou envious against the workers of iniquity. For they shall soon be cut down like the grass, and wither as the green herb. Commit thy way unto the Lord; trust also in him; and he shall bring it to pass.

–Psalm 37:1–2, 5

Please, Lord, step into this situation. I don't know what to do. Things were done, words were said, and now I'm at odds with someone. Maybe I was wrong, but I don't think so. Honestly, I want to blame the other person for all of it, but maybe I have a blind spot. I want to sort things out and turn things around, but I'm not sure where to start. I don't know if a half-baked apology will do any good, especially if I don't really mean it. And actually, I should be receiving an apology, but I doubt that will ever happen. I beg you, please do your work here. Shine your light so we see things clearly. Use your power to dismantle whatever grudges we have piled up. I commit this whole mess to you.

Call unto me, and I will answer thee, and show thee great and mighty things, which thou knowest not.

—Jeremiah 33:3

God, we know that pain has produced some wisdom in our lives, but it has also created cynicism and fear. People turn on us, reject us, hurt us, and none of us wants to play the fool more than once, so we're tempted to close off our hearts to people and to you. But relationships that bring meaning and joy require vulnerability. Help us trust you to be our truest friend and to lead us to the kind of community that will bring healing rather than destruction.

Wealth maketh many friends; but the poor is separated from his neighbour.

—Proverbs 19:4

Lord, I live in an increasingly tiered society, in which people associate only with others of similar income. I am grateful to be solidly middle class, with all the opportunity that affords me and my family, and I take pride in my ability to provide for my loved ones. Yet I must remember not to let economics alone inform my relationships with others. The type of car I drive or the size of my home are hollow gauges for who I am as a person; to judge or be judged based on this criteria is not only shallow, but foolhardy.

God, help me to remember to choose my friends wisely, honoring the qualities that matter—integrity, creativity, wisdom, a sense of justice, and kindness—rather than a person's wealth or status.

Henceforth I call you not servants; for the servant knoweth not what his lord doeth: but I have called you friends; for all things that I have heard of my Father I have made known unto you.

–John 15:15

God wants trusted friends for us. One of the things Daniel appreciates about his long-standing friendship with Kevin is that the two can be open with one another. "I share everything with Kevin," Daniel says. "When I went through my divorce, I was very angry, and Kevin was someone I could talk to without censoring myself. He does not judge me. Kevin knows my weaknesses as well as my strengths, and he still has my back!"

Dear Lord, may I follow the example of Jesus and share openly and completely with trusted friends.

Where no counsel is, the people fall: but in the multitude of counselors there is safety.

—Proverbs 11:14

Nate has always prided himself on his independence. But when buying a new home, he sought the advice of trusted friends: Ken, who works in construction and could spot structural issues, and Denise, who has a good head for finance and helped Nate navigate the paperwork. With their support, he found a solid house at a price he could afford. "It's hard for me to rely on others," Nate confessed. "But my friends helped me make a wise choice."

Dear Lord, grant me the humility to seek—and listen to!—the counsel of others. Grant me the wisdom to surround myself with wise friends.

And they continued stedfastly in the apostles' doctrine and fellowship, and in breaking of bread, and in prayers.

—Acts 2:42

When I was a boy, my mom used to talk about "refilling the well," by which she meant the joy she took in being with people who filled her up—who restored her. I thought of her expression last week, when I had lunch with an old classmate; when he and I parted, I was struck by how being with this friend energized rather than depleted me. He is a calm, spiritual person, and our times together never fail to leave me feeling uplifted. Our conversations are wide-ranging and thoughtful, and my friend is a person with whom I feel comfortable sharing my spiritual musings. He and I challenge one another; we don't always agree, but our relationship is such that we inspire one another to learn and grow.

Lord, may I remember the importance of developing relationships with other believers, whose fellowship and spiritual life can help to deepen my faith.

A friend loveth at all times, and a brother is born for adversity.

—Proverbs 17:17

Ralph's grandfather would say, "Welcome challenging times, and see who your friends are." Ralph experienced that firsthand when he became caregiver for his ailing dad. Over time, he learned who thought of his friendship as a priority: some relationships faded because Ralph's schedule was no longer as flexible. It was painful to realize that not all his friendships were as close as he'd thought, but looking back now, Ralph appreciates—and celebrates—the friends who stuck by him.

God, thank you for those friends who love and support us through hard times.

Father, it's easy to say, "Let me know if there's anything I can do." But how much better to peer closer, assess the situation to find what needs doing...then simply do it. Help me look into a friend's needs instead of waiting to be asked. Help me replace the words I utter so glibly with actions that might matter even more. Amen.

A faithful friend is an image of God.

–French Proverb

> *He that covereth a transgression seeketh love; but he that repeateth a matter separateth very friends.*
>
> –Proverbs 17:9

I have a flexible job that allows me to work at home, but a couple days a week, I drive in to the office. I like my coworkers, but because I don't see them every day, I feel the need to work harder to stay connected with them. Staying connected is a worthy goal, but lately I've developed a tendency to draw others close via gossip and sardonic commentary on other colleagues. Wanting to "get the dirt" on others is a human tendency, and I've exploited that, leavening my observations with humor so as to come across in what I've liked to think is a likable fashion. In fact, I took pride in my reputation for being caustic and funny, until the other day, when a new hire approached me and said, only half joking, "I hear I need to stay on your good side!" Her comment made me see myself in a different light, and I feel compelled to make some changes in my approach to the workplace.

Dear Lord, teach me the wisdom of exercising good judgment and not gossiping about the shortcomings of others.

> *I will not leave you comfortless: I will come to you.*
>
> —John 14:18

My mom died of cancer when I was still in college. She was diagnosed with a brain tumor in the spring, and was gone before Christmas. My dad was devastated and in his grief, withdrew from the world; he could not be there for us kids to lean on emotionally. It was a very difficult time in my life; what got me through was the support I received at the church in my college town. In what was probably the loneliest time in my life, I was nevertheless surrounded by love. Various members of the congregation invited me over for home-cooked meals or pizza-and-movie nights. These folks encouraged me that God was still there, and through their loving actions, I experienced God's grace. God is with us even when we feel alone.

The hoary head is a crown of glory, if it be found in the way of righteousness.

–Proverbs 16:31

Over the years, my siblings and I have sometimes drifted apart, not through animosity but because we've all been busy with our own immediate families. In dealing with our parents as they age and develop some health problems, we've moved back into a shared orbit.

Thank you, God, for that newfound closeness as we navigate these sometimes daunting challenges together.

Honour thy father and thy mother: that thy days may be long upon the land which the Lord thy God giveth thee.

–Exodus 20:12

CHAPTER 13
HEAVEN

Set your affection on things above, not on things on the earth.

–Colossians 3:2

But rather seek ye the kingdom of God; and all these things shall be added unto you.

–Luke 12:31

Last summer, my wife and I took a road trip out West. We drove from Chicago to Seattle, taking primarily two-lane roads, and making our route up as we went along. I will never forget the evening we pulled into a little town in South Dakota. It was dinnertime, that golden hour when the sunlight looks like thick yellow syrup. As we drove, the fields around us were drenched in a honey-colored light. "This must be what heaven is like," my wife remarked, nodding at a great round lake on the outskirts of town. It almost appeared to be gilded. Her observation filled me with joy–and hope. I was reminded that by setting our sights on God's kingdom, we achieve a blessing in this life.

> *Nevertheless we, according to his promise, look for new heavens and a new earth, wherein dwelleth righteousness.*
>
> –2 Peter 3:13

Life can be challenging. It is imperfect. It can be ugly. I commute to work by train, and sometimes the litter I see by the side of the tracks saddens me—papers, plastic bags, abandoned toys, even once the rusted hulk of a car. We are not always good stewards of the world we live in, and while I believe it is important that we continue to try to repair and care for our earthly home, I also take comfort in the assurance of a shining life after this one. "New heavens and a new earth": that promise fills me with hope.

Lord, thank you for reminding me that all will be made anew!

Sing the wondrous love of Jesus,
Sing his mercy and his grace;
In the mansions bright and blessed,
He'll prepare for us a place.
While we walk the pilgrim pathway,
Clouds will overspread the sky;
But when trav'ling days are over,
Not a shadow, not a sigh.
When we all get to heaven,
What a day of rejoicing that will be!
When we all see Jesus,
We'll sing and shout the victory.

–Eliza E. Hewitt,
"When We All Get To Heaven"

For God so loved the world, that he gave his only begotten Son, that whosoever believeth in him should not perish, but have everlasting life.

–John 3:16

I am a hospice nurse, and have seen in my work how the instinct to cling to life is strong. As a Christian, I believe that I can look forward to everlasting life after my time on Earth, but I imagine that when my time does come, it will be hard to let go of the life I know, populated by those I love. It is ironic and yet compelling that we cling to a temporary life on Earth, which is but a glimmer of what eternal life in heaven will be.

Lord, help me to appreciate the transient beauty of life on Earth, even as I remember and embrace your promise of heaven and life everlasting.

But none of these things move me, neither count I my life dear unto myself, so that I might finish my course with joy, and the ministry, which I have received of the Lord Jesus, to testify the gospel of the grace of God.

–Acts 20:24

We are products of our environment. I learned from my parents, who learned from their parents, and it is not just what children hear–it is what they see, day in and day out. My parents were good people. They are both deceased, but I believe they are in heaven. I also believe it is my responsibility to live in such a way that carries on their legacy of dignity and grace. I can model that behavior for my own children, teens now, and in so doing inspire them to choose a life informed by Christ's teachings. It is an awesome responsibility to live in such a way that others are inspired to seek the joy of heaven.

In my Father's house are many mansions: if it were not so, I would have told you. I go to prepare a place for you.

–John 14:2

When I was a child, I imagined heaven to be an impersonal, abstract place, perhaps filled with fluffy white clouds, and harps, and singing angels. Somehow heaven lacked the comfort and warmth of my own bedroom, with its unique touches such as my favorite books and toys. Now that I am grown, I am no longer certain of what heaven will be like. Is it a "place" in the sense that I know: a field, or forest, or grassy knoll? Or is it unlike anything I have experienced in this lifetime? I cannot imagine, but heaven feels more personal to me when I remember the Biblical promise that there is a spot for me there–which the Lord has prepared! Now I wonder, what personal touches await?

Lord, thank you for preparing an individual place for me in heaven.

But the wisdom that is from above is first pure, then peaceable, gentle, and easy to be intreated, full of mercy and good fruits, without partiality, and without hypocrisy.

–James 3:17

When I read this verse, I realize how perfectly Jesus personified heavenly wisdom. It's a wonder to me that we are called to walk in his footsteps, but then I remember that it is only possible to do it through the Spirit that works in and through us.

Thank you, Lord, for making the things of heaven available to those who seek them.

Verily, verily, I say unto you, He that believeth on me hath everlasting life. I am that bread of life. Your fathers did eat manna in the wilderness, and are dead. This is the bread which cometh down from heaven, that a man may eat thereof, and not die. I am the living bread which came down from heaven: if any man eat of this bread, he shall live for ever: and the bread that I will give is my flesh, which I will give for the life of the world.

–John 6:47–51

Nothing fills us like the bread from heaven. Jesus says here there is spiritual food: lasting and alive. He is himself the bread of life, the bread that satisfies us in this life and the next one. The eternal life that he gives is costly, though. He gives his own flesh for the life of the world, a life that does not end. Believe in me, he says. That's the bread of life.

Heaven is not reached at a single bound;
But we build the ladder by which we rise
From the lowly earth to the vaulted skies,
And we mount to its summit round by round.

—Josiah Gilbert Holland

When we remember that we are working for the rewards of heaven and not for the praise of people, we are able to press on and persevere in the tasks ahead of us.

CHAPTER 14
FATHERHOOD

And, ye fathers, provoke not your children to wrath: but bring them up in the nurture and admonition of the Lord.

—Ephesians 6:4

And not only so, but we glory in tribulations also: knowing that tribulation worketh patience.

–Romans 5:3

As a father, what I wish for my daughter Anne is an easy path. When she struggles with her studies or experiences conflicts with friends, my heart aches. I know, however, that no one can be shielded from pain indefinitely, and that it is adversity as well as our joys and successes that shape us. My grandfather used to say that misfortune can build character, and I see that in my daughter: challenges have shown her that she possesses an inner steel, even as they've demanded she develop patience and compassion.

Dear Lord, help me to guide Anne so that she might meet hardship with strength, patience, and grace. May adversity help her to grow as a person.

And he arose, and came to his father. But when he was yet a great way off, his father saw him, and had compassion, and ran, and fell on his neck, and kissed him. And the son said unto him, Father, I have sinned against heaven, and in thy sight, and am no more worthy to be called thy son.

–Luke 15:20–21

I love the story of the prodigal son. It reminds me of the bond parents and children share, and it reminds me of the simple fact that our children are human. They are going to make mistakes; sometimes they are going to disappoint us, deeply. But as parents, we are called upon to love our children, and forgive them, even when they have hurt us. (God, I suppose you know exactly what I mean: even when I make mistakes, your love for me remains a constant.)

Dear Lord, may I have the strength and wisdom to always love my children and be there for them, even when they disobey.

By faith Moses, when he was born, was hid three months of his parents, because they saw he was a proper child; and they were not afraid of the king's commandment.

–Hebrews 11:23

Dear Lord, my role as a parent puts me in a commanding position. Children have little power, and it is up to me, as my child's guardian, to be a protector and advocate in a world that is not always just. My son, who is nine, has been dealing with a bully at school. I've had to go in to meet with the principal and the other boy's parents several times, and the parents have on more than one occasion grown belligerent. It's an uncomfortable situation, but I know I must remain strong and level headed in order to support my child.

God, please grant me the strength to always do what is right for my child, even at risk of personal discomfort, as the parents of Moses did.

Children, obey your parents in all things: for this is well pleasing unto the Lord.

–Colossians 3:20

Dear Lord, I am officially in the "Sandwich Generation," raising my own children while helping my parents navigate the challenges of aging. Mom and Dad, who have always been there for me, now need me in new ways. Dad has developed Parkinson's, and Mom's arthritis is getting worse. My wife and I are devoted to helping them with practical matters like getting to the doctor, cleaning their home, and buying groceries, and I have recently started bringing my older daughter along when we run errands with Mom. The challenges my folks face make me keenly aware of life's cycles of loss and change; I know my daughter feels it, too. But my hope is that these dates with Mom might be a way to demonstrate to my daughter what respect for elders can mean. Aging is a part of being, and compassion is an important lesson.

Dear God, help me set the right example for my children through my relationship with my own parents.

Now his parents went to Jerusalem every year at the feast of the passover.

–Luke 2:41

My wife, two children, and I recently took a road trip to Boston. My middle school son has been studying the American Revolution, and Boston's rich history and wealth of museums drew us. We had a wonderful time exploring the city, but an unanticipated pleasure was the time it took to drive from our Midwestern home to the East Coast and back again. In the car, we read, talked, and listened to music. Upon our return home, we felt refreshed and connected, and my son mentioned that the next time we travel, he hopes we drive again. As he put it: "It'll be our tradition, you know?" The next day we went to church together, and I felt that same connection.

Lord, I am reminded of the importance of family traditions—like going on road trips or worshipping together—and the bonds and continuity they foster. Please grant me the creativity to pursue traditions that enrich my family life; may I never lose sight of their importance.

His parents answered them and said, We know that this is our son, and that he was born blind.

–John 9:20

Our friend's daughter has been having problems at school. Because of social and academic challenges the girl faces, her parents have elected to pull her from public school and pursue home schooling. The change mandates major adjustments on the part of the entire family. My friend's wife has quit her job to be at home with their daughter, effecting a change in her own goals and in the family's finances. When my friend shared their decision with me, my kneejerk reaction–though fortunately I did not voice it–was one of judgment. Public school was good enough for my kids; why wasn't it good enough for this girl? But as my friend and I talked, and I became aware of the emotional difficulties the young woman faces, I began to appreciate the choice my friend and his wife have made, even with its attendant sacrifices. We do what we can to support our children, and people's strengths and needs vary.

God, you have blessed me with healthy children, and I thank you. But my kids are human beings, with their own needs, and my wife and I do not hesitate to make the decisions that best support them. Please help me be sensitive to the parents of children with special needs, and respectful of their decisions and life journey.

Lord, it is so hard to build a sense of responsibility in some children. Each child reacts so differently to chores. One gets them done right away with no grumbling, while another dawdles and accomplishes nothing. I don't want to be just a scorekeeper, keeping track of who does what. I want my children to learn the value of carrying part of the responsibility for our family's comfort.

Give me the wisdom to develop in each child a healthy respect for their work and for the way it fits into a larger plan for the good of all. You value work, Lord. Instill in my youngsters a desire to carry part of the load and to feel pride in the accomplishment.

Have not I commanded thee? Be strong and of a good courage; be not afraid, neither be thou dismayed: for the Lord thy God is with thee whithersoever thou goest.

–Joshua 1:9

Dear Lord, my daughter's school life has been miserable lately. For the past four years, she and two other girls have been inseparable. Birthday parties, sleepovers, movie dates: when two of them gather, it's been a given that the third will be invited to join. We've even vacationed with the other girls' families! But this year, something changed: a new girl joined the group, and my daughter has started to feel marginalized. Last week, the other three went shopping and "forgot" to invite her. When she went to a sleepover, the other girls had a series of private jokes to which my daughter wasn't privy. My heart bleeds for her, and sometimes I have a hard time masking my own anger at the situation.

God, please help me to remain strong so that I can be there for my girl; may I help my daughter navigate these difficulties with grace.

Train up a child in the way he should go: and when he is old, he will not depart from it.

—Proverbs 22:6

Lord, I tried to teach my children the way to go. Sometimes I didn't get it right. Now it is up to you. May your Spirit bring to their minds those things they learned about you and your Word. May these truths guide them as they make their own choices and build their own relationships. Help me to rest in your promise, even when I can't see it happening. Yet.

Lo, children are an heritage of the Lord; and the fruit of the womb is his reward.

—Psalm 127:3

How can I thank you enough for my wife and children? When I step back from everyday concerns for a moment, I am overwhelmed with appreciation. We all have our flaws and sins, but you've given us a home full of love for each other. Please protect us from harm, guide us in your paths towards wisdom, and bless us abundantly.

Judge not, that ye be not judged.

—Matthew 7:1

Dear Lord, I have a daughter in middle school. She and her friends are coming into their own, trying to figure out who they are. Technology makes it even simpler to be unkind, and it is tempting to adopt a judgmental attitude in order to fit in with others. God, help me guide my children as they navigate this time of change and growth. Please protect my family from the ways of the judgmental, and from adopting those ways in our interactions with others.

Let Israel rejoice in him that made him: let the children of Zion be joyful in their King.

–Psalm 149:2

Lord, I suppose in every family there is a child whose self-esteem suffers by comparison with siblings. Let me be sensitive to the subtle messages my children are receiving within the family circle, regarding their self-worth. Help me to show my confidence in each child and to remind them all that they matter to our family. They also matter to you, Lord, for you are the God who cares for and values each of your children. Give my young ones the assurance that comes with knowing they are the children of a King.

Seest thou how faith wrought with his works, and by works was faith made perfect?

—James 2:22

Dear Lord, teach my children to follow my lead in actions and deeds and to model my behavior more so than my words. Often I speak in frustration, but I always act in patience, kindness, and love. I want the same for my children. Help them do as I do, not as I say. Help my wife see beyond my occasional sharp or impatient words, my words of confusion, fear, and annoyance when things aren't going the way I would like. Help her to see the love I give, the work I do, the way I live and move and have my being. Amen.

God, children have the most amazing capacity for loyalty; they look to their parents with trust that all will be well. Sometimes I fear that I cannot live up to the faith that my children put in me, that I am not as strong or as invincible as they believe me to be. Lord, help me appreciate their trust as the privilege that it is. Help me to be a rock for my little ones, even as you are a rock for me. You see into my heart; you know the strength and fear that exist side by side within it. Guide me—helping me access the strength I possess and the strength you give freely—as I strive to create a stable and loving home for my family.

The promise is unto you, and to your children, and to all that are afar off, even as many as the Lord our God shall call.

—Acts 2:39

Lord, how we cling to your promise that the Holy Spirit is always near to all who believe in you. How comforting it is for us as parents to know that our children have the Holy Spirit to guide them and lead them into a purposeful life. We praise you, Lord, for your loving care for us and for our children and grandchildren.

CHAPTER 15
GENEROSITY

He coveteth greedily all the day long: but the righteous giveth and spareth not.

—Proverbs 21:26

But this I say, He which soweth sparingly shall reap also sparingly; and he which soweth bountifully shall reap also bountifully.

–2 Corinthians 9:6

In discussing their giving to the Lord's work, the Apostle Paul tells the people of the church in Corinth to give regularly and cheerfully. He also tells them to give generously. If they sow bountifully, they will reap bountifully. It is pretty clear we can't outgive God, whose resources and generosity are infinitely greater than our own. So don't be stingy, especially when it comes to kingdom purposes.

I exhort therefore, that, first of all, supplications, prayers, intercessions, and giving of thanks, be made for all men.

–1 Timothy 2:1

Dear Lord, I live in a time and place of entitlement. Sometimes, when others are kind to me, generously offering their time or assistance, I am in such a hurry that I take their kindness as no more than my due. My neighbor set aside his own work to help me when I struggled in building a prefab kitchen island equipped with hard-to-decipher directions; my sister took off work and traveled far to attend my son's middle school graduation. Now I have a sturdy piece of furniture, and my son's day was enriched by the presence and support of his aunt.

God, these acts of love deserve to be recognized as such. Please help me to remember to slow down, appreciate, and thank those who are generous to me.

Whoso stoppeth his ears at the cry of the poor, he also shall cry himself, but shall not be heard.

—Proverbs 21:13

My wife and I work hard, but some months money is tight. We have become adept at cutting costs, and although we will never be what our culture considers wealthy, I am grateful that we have what we need. The other day, I read about the devastating flooding in Louisiana, and was reminded of how generosity can manifest itself in different ways. While we can donate a small amount of cash, I also, perhaps more crucially, can devote some of my time to volunteer efforts. I am healthy and can even donate blood.

God, I am blessed in so many ways; please help me to remember the importance of generosity, and how it can take many forms.

Every man according as he purposeth in his heart, so let him give; not grudgingly, or of necessity: for God loveth a cheerful giver.

–2 Corinthians 9:7

My wife is a nurse, and lately the hospital where she works has been short-staffed. Though new hires will soon be brought onboard, for the time being, my wife's schedule is more taxing. When I promised her I would pick up the slack at home, including taking on more of the cooking and cleaning, I was sincere. And yet, yesterday I was tired and ungraciously reminded my wife of all I was doing. Her face fell, and I was ashamed; here we are, both working so hard, and I spoiled my kind efforts with bitterness! I have since made amends, but dear Lord, please remind me to give with good cheer, not grumbling.

He doth execute the judgment of the fatherless and widow, and loveth the stranger, in giving him food and raiment.

–Deuteronomy 10:18

When I was a boy, my Sunday School teacher encouraged us, one week, to keep track of the kind things we did for others. I prepared a careful ledger, describing the dishes I washed for my mom after dinner, the popcorn I shared with my younger brother. The next Sunday, I proudly showed my list to the teacher. He praised my efforts, which pleased me greatly. I looked up to this man the way I looked up to my own father. We talked about how important it is to do kindnesses for the ones we love, and then he said, "And the next step, son, is to serve those we don't even know!" He explained that while it takes just that little bit more effort to extend ourselves for strangers, that is Christ's way.

Dear Lord, all these years later, those words have stayed with me; may I be generous to strangers, not just to those I know and love.

And when she had done giving him drink, she said, I will draw water for thy camels also, until they have done drinking.

–Genesis 24:19

Life is busy. And sometimes I am so caught up in the demands of the day (get the kids to school, work, pick up the dry cleaning) that I forget the importance of slowing down and favoring generosity of spirit over efficiency. Just yesterday, I was racing through the grocery store; I'd promised my wife I'd pick up some meat for dinner, and as I rushed down the aisle I heard someone call my name. It was my daughter's kindergarten teacher, an older lady who, even standing on tiptoe, barely clears my shoulder. She smiled at me and asked if I could reach up and grab a few cans from the top shelf. My first reaction, which I hope I suppressed, was annoyance; I was in a hurry, after all! But I stopped, and this lady was so grateful, and she complimented my daughter (which of course endeared me to her), so that I was still warmed by the encounter as I paid for my groceries. I even felt inspired to crack a joke with the bagger, a raw-faced kid I'd never noticed before, and when I got home, I made a point of asking my daughter about school—I even invited her to "help" me unpack the groceries. Five-year-olds aren't very efficient, but the time we shared was worth far more than an orderly fridge. I reflected later how those encounters and the mindful connection they provided filled my own spirit. Opening myself to generosity can be like cracking open a door on stiff hinges, but once I do, and the light shines in, it gets easier and easier to throw the door wide to more opportunity.

God, help me remember that one generous act begets another. Help me remember to take that first step, because when I do, I benefit as much as those to whom I've reached out.

Give, and it shall be given unto you; good measure, pressed down, and shaken together, and running over, shall men give into your bosom. For with the same measure that ye mete withal it shall be measured to you again.

–Luke 6:38

We all have something to offer: time, money, expertise. God exhorts us to give generously; in his infinite wisdom, he understands that when we give, we're not just helping others (worthy in and of itself). But we also help ourselves. Studies have shown that generosity helps to manage personal stress, and have linked unselfishness and giving with a general sense of life satisfaction and a lower risk of early death. When we reach outside ourselves, we connect with others; God wants that connection, that sense of purpose and happiness, for each of us.

Dear Lord, help us to connect with our best selves; help us to be generous givers.

Bring ye all the tithes into the storehouse, that there may be meat in mine house, and prove me now herewith, saith the Lord of hosts, if I will not open you the windows of heaven, and pour you out a blessing, that there shall not be room enough to receive it.

–Malachi 3:10

God proves himself by being generous to generous people. If our actions reflect and imitate his, he opens the windows of heaven and pours out blessings on us. Everywhere you go is his storehouse, and everyone you meet bears his image. So quit pinching your pennies. Be generous, and the blessings you receive will be too numerous to count.

Being enriched in every thing to all bountifulness, which causeth through us thanksgiving to God.

—2 Corinthians 9:11

Pitching in on the caregiving rotation for my elderly uncle was not something I initially perceived as a blessing, but as a gift I was giving to my uncle and my cousin. Still, God, I thank you for this opportunity to grow, to give, and to learn. The work of caregiving can be stressful and emotionally wearing, but I am learning that when I trust in you and let you work through me, I am able to do the work with a generous heart.

All our opportunities, abilities, and resources come from God. They are given to us to hold in sacred trust for him. Cooperating with God will permit us to generously pass on to others some of the many blessings from his rich storehouse.

Lord, grant me a simple, kind, open, believing, loving and generous heart, worthy of being your dwelling place.

–John Sergieff

And he said, Of a truth I say unto you, that this poor widow hath cast in more than they all: For all these have of their abundance cast in unto the offerings of God: but she of her penury hath cast in all the living that she had.

–Luke 21:3–4

I ask you for a spirit of both generosity and trust. Generosity prompts us to want to share what we have with others, to take care of our neighbors. Trust lets us believe that you will take care of us and provide our daily bread. When I am blessed with abundance, let me give with abundance. And when I feel scarcity, let me give anyway.

Blessed are they which do hunger and thirst after righteousness: for they shall be filled.

—Matthew 5:6

There's so much injustice in this world. There are so many people hurting because of other people's carelessness, selfishness, or desire for power and wealth at other people's expense. Please grant me a giving, generous heart when it comes to treating people fairly, to taking care of the widow and orphan, and to acting justly. When it becomes overwhelming, please help me discern where my efforts can do the most good in righting wrongs in my social circles and my community.

CHAPTER 16

FAITH

For we walk by faith, not by sight.

–2 Corinthians 5:7

Rejoice, and be exceeding glad: for great is your reward in heaven: for so persecuted they the prophets which were before you.

—Matthew 5:12

When my courage wavers, when it would be difficult to witness to my faith, let me be inspired by the faith of those who came before me. Hold me fast to my convictions, God, so I may honor you and not stray from your path.

> *For therein is the righteousness of God revealed from faith to faith: as it is written, The just shall live by faith.*
>
> –Romans 1:17

Faith is more than a passive idea; it is a principle of action that motivates our day-to-day decisions and actions. Would a farmer plant if he did not expect to harvest? Would the student read and study if she did not believe it would improve the quality of her life? Would we work hard each day if we did not hope that by doing so we might accomplish something worthwhile?

We daily act upon things we believe in, though we cannot yet see the end result. This is the faith we live by, whether we identify it as such or not.

As faithful people, we take this principle one step further: we do things that are motivated by our faith in things promised but not yet fulfilled. We smile in the face of adversity. We continue in prayer even when our prayers don't seem to be answered. We stop saying, "I can't" and start believing God can! Step by step, we put our faith into action and learn to "live by faith."

And brought in the offerings and the tithes and the dedicated things faithfully: over which Cononiah the Levite was ruler, and Shimei his brother was the next.

–2 Chronicles 31:12

Dear God, money is tight: our old refrigerator gave out sooner than we might have hoped and replacing it was an unexpected expense, as was the series of doctor's visits when I strained my shoulder. Last Sunday, the ushers passed the offering plate and I am ashamed to admit that I held back: after all, I justified, I am spread thin this month! Rather than contributing something, I contributed nothing, and in my frugality, I lost both connection and the sense of continuity I strive for in my spiritual life. Lord, giving to you is not only an act of faith (because I am giving to someone unseen), but also something I should do faithfully. Thank you for helping me to remember this.

Then Ahimelech answered the king, and said, And who is so faithful among all thy servants as David, which is the king's son in law, and goeth at thy bidding, and is honourable in thine house?

–1 Samuel 22:14

I have traditionally thought of faith as a way to keep strong my personal connection to God. But this week I found myself in conversation with a new workmate, an atheist, who asked me point blank whether I believe in God. When I avowed that I do, my companion asked what sustains that conviction, to which I replied simply, "Faith." That night, as I reviewed the conversation, I felt relief that I had made clear my beliefs. To downplay them, I realized, would have felt like a betrayal. In that moment I was struck by the revolutionary idea that God wants us to be faithful simply to . . . serve him.

Dear Lord, help me to remember that faith is more than a means of strengthening my relationship with you–it's also a way of serving you.

Wherefore I put thee in remembrance that thou stir up the gift of God, which is in thee by the putting on of my hands. For God hath not given us the spirit of fear; but of power, and of love, and of a sound mind.

—2 Timothy 1:6–7

Faith and fear cannot coexist. One always gives way to the other. It is necessary for us to be constantly building up our faith to overcome the numerous sources of destructive disbelief all around us. We need to be continually working at rekindling the gift of God that is in us, which is our faith in him and in his promises. We must be dedicated to developing a spirit of love and power and discipline within ourselves. Studying the words of the scriptures, meditating on them, keeping God's commandments, and praying daily are some of the ways we can keep our faith strong. By focusing on these things, we shut out fear and cultivate faith.

My servant Moses is not so, who is faithful in all mine house.

–Numbers 12:7

I miss my parents, both of whom died within the last 10 years, but each day I strive to keep them alive—in my heart and in the world—by emulating the way they lived their lives. On days when I struggle, I remember my mother's kindness, my father's acts of service. I remember the day my dad and I shared coffee and talked about the qualities he admired in others: "Faith," he said, without hesitation. "Faith in God, in one's own path. From faith springs generosity of spirit." He went on to say that in the Bible, the stories of faith as embodied by men such as Moses uplifted him.

Dear God, may I persevere and have faith. Help me to remember that faithfulness is an attribute of great men like Moses, and within my reach as I strive to be my best self.

Lord, perfect for me what is lacking of thy gifts; of faith, help thou mine unbelief; of hope, establish my trembling hope; of love, kindle its smoking flax.

–Lancelot Andrewes

Faith is a true sign of bravery. It is looking forward to the future despite challenges and adversity; it is trusting in something that you can neither see nor touch yet knowing it is always there guiding you along life's path.

Now faith is the substance of things hoped for, the evidence of things not seen.

–Hebrews 11:1

My daughter has a child's Bible, and she loves the stories about Jesus and the miracles he wrought: water into wine, healing the sick. "Dad, why don't we see miracles like this anymore?" she asked me just yesterday. Her question echoed a wish I have had on more than one occasion: living in a society so bent on flash, on the next best thing, I myself have yearned to see visible signs of God's presence. But as my daughter and I talked, we began to acknowledge the presence of miracles in the everyday: the antibiotic she took last week for an ear infection; the rosemary seeds we'd planted together, which are gaining traction and sprouting up. Health and new life burgeon behind the scenes: our world is, in fact, full of miracles! And when we cannot recognize them for the miracles they are? Then we must rely on faith.

God, help me to see the miracles in my life, and strengthen me to have faith even when I don't see visible signs of your presence.

And he said, The things which are impossible with men are possible with God.

–Luke 18:27

Only faith can look past a seemingly impossible situation and believe that it will change. I believe you are a God of miracles, Lord. These are days of miracles, as were the days of Noah, Moses, and Joseph. I may not see the seas parted, peoples freed, or congregations caught up to heaven, but through faith I expect wonderful gifts from you. I believe that with you, all things are possible!

Know therefore that the Lord thy God, he is God, the faithful God, which keepeth covenant and mercy with them that love him and keep his commandments to a thousand generations.

–Deuteronomy 7:9

Today I found out that a close friend has been diagnosed with pancreatic cancer. Dear God, this man was healthy. He kept fit and he ate a good diet. His family is devastated, and I am reminded of how quickly our lives can change. God, some change makes me afraid, and in the face of my fear, I must remember to have faith in you. I must never lose sight of the fact that you keep the faith for me, also; you are there for me. I can share my fears with you. I can unburden myself. I can ask you how to best support my friend and his loved ones.

Dear God, please help me to remember that faith is a two-way street: even as I work to remain faithful to you and all you stand for, you are faithful to me, and I can take comfort in that fact.

God is faithful, by whom ye were called unto the fellowship of his Son Jesus Christ our Lord.

–1 Corinthians 1:9

Last year, an old college friend called with the devastating news that after 23 years of marriage, his wife had admitted to a long-standing affair and asked for a divorce. My friend had felt secure in his wife's love, and was blindsided by this betrayal. In the months since, he has taken comfort in the community of his church, and found solace in his faith. "It's true: sometimes people disappoint us," he told me recently. We'd met for lunch, and though he spoke wryly, he looked and sounded better than he had in months. "But God is always faithful to us." I was struck by his words, and on the walk home pondered the resilience that grows when we know someone has our back.

Dear Lord, help me to remember that you are a constant in my life, in times of joy but also adversity.

Hearken, my beloved brethren, Hath not God chosen the poor of this world rich in faith, and heirs of the kingdom which he hath promised to them that love him?

–James 2:5

Jesus taught that it is often difficult for a rich man to enter heaven. That's because they don't feel like they need anything. But here he says the poor are often rich in faith and thus heirs to his kingdom. This is not because they are more virtuous, but precisely because they are more needy. They turn to God in faith and love him because he loved them first. They know they need him, which is where true faith starts. Sometimes it is hard to see that if you don't need anything.

Let us hold fast the profession of our faith without wavering; (for he is faithful that promised).

—Hebrews 10:23

Simon and his wife Jessica moved to their new home during winter, and he'd looked forward to the neighborhood's annual summer block party. Simon figured he'd meet new people; what he didn't anticipate was that his faith might be challenged. "So you're one of those religious types?" a woman laughed, upon learning that Simon and Jessica attended a church nearby. Though uncomfortable, Simon dug deep: "Yes," he responded with polite firmness. "We've found happiness in our new church home."

Dear Lord, sometimes I am asked to justify my faith; sometimes I am even mocked for it. Please strengthen my heart and give me the right words and spirit to articulate my belief.

Above all, taking the shield of faith, wherewith ye shall be able to quench all the fiery darts of the wicked.

—Ephesians 6:16

Today I face a frightening health issue, God, and I am more afraid than I would like to admit. Nobody wants illness. Nobody wants to go under the knife or be told they may not live to see their children grow up. But I have you, God, and with your presence today, I know I can get through any challenge. I know I can stand up to the fear and the worry and vanquish it with love and faith. I know you don't give me more than I can handle, God, and that you'll be there to handle it with me nonetheless. Thank you, God, for being my shield and my rock and my faithful warrior.

And now abideth faith, hope, charity, these three; but the greatest of these is charity.

—1 Corinthians 13:13

My heavenly Father, what do I have to fear when you are the one caring for me? And yet, I do fear; irrationally I fear, despite your faithfulness, despite your assurances, and despite your promises. Why do I still fear? I don't always understand my trembling heart and the shadows of things far smaller than you before which it cowers. Please liberate me from these lapses of trust. Free me to stand fearlessly, supported by faith and hope, in the center of your great love for me.

> *And I say unto you, Ask, and it shall be given you; seek, and ye shall find; knock, and it shall be opened unto you. For every one that asketh receiveth; and he that seeketh findeth; and to him that knocketh it shall be opened.*
>
> –Luke 11:9–10

Lord, I know you will show your goodness and faithfulness to me if I just diligently seek you. The problem isn't your willingness to give, but my tendency to try to do everything by myself rather than leaning on and trusting in you. This silly inclination brings me needless stress and wastes precious time. Today I endeavor to lay my needs and troubles at your feet the minute I begin to feel the least bit overwhelmed.

But without faith it is impossible to please him: for he that cometh to God must believe that he is, and that he is a rewarder of them that diligently seek him.

—Hebrews 11:6

Only a few things are actually impossible. And this is one of them: to please God without faith, not faith in ourselves, but faith in him. We have to believe he exists, and that he rewards us for simply believing in him and desiring him. The reward, of course, is that we find him. This is what pleases him, that we would receive our hope and satisfaction in him. This is what has always pleased him, from Abraham until today: people who seek him with humility and joy.

CHAPTER 17
JOY

Thou wilt shew me the path of life: in thy presence is fulness of joy; at thy right hand there are pleasures for evermore.

–Psalm 16:11

And these things write we unto you, that your joy may be full.

–1 John 1:4

My mother was a joyful person. She faced challenges like everyone else—her health in particular troubled her off and on through most of her adult life—but as a rule, she chose to focus on the positive. Her joyful outlook took many forms—she was a calm, good listener; she embraced new experiences; she was interested and interesting. And something that strikes me now is how her radiant spirit was often contagious. I myself would sometimes return from school glum or discouraged, but if we spent some quiet time together—working in the garden, say, or sometimes I would finish my homework in the kitchen while Mom cooked dinner—my own spirits lifted. Mom died last year, and as an adult, I am left to carry her bright torch for my own family.

God, help me to always remember how important it is to share our joy with others so that they may experience it.

But the fruit of the Spirit is love, joy, peace, longsuffering, gentleness, goodness, faith.

—Galatians 5:22

As an adult with many demands on my time and energy, I am always interested in how to consistently achieve my potential and be my best self. For many years, I've enjoyed swimming as a way to stay healthy, both physically and emotionally. After a long day, a good swim clears my head, tones my muscles, and keeps me sharp and upbeat. Similarly, I've found that staying spiritually active has a positive effect on my outlook. Like exercise, staying spiritually engaged takes discipline—and sometimes I would rather just sit on the couch and eat chips! But when I make the effort, physical and spiritual exercise helps me to realize joy.

Lord, please may I always remember that happiness can be part of the package when I develop my spiritual muscle. I can "work at" making joy a constant in my life.

And ye now therefore have sorrow: but I will see you again, and your heart shall rejoice, and your joy no man taketh from you.

–John 16:22

Life has its difficult chapters. In the past two years, both my parents died and my beloved son struggled with his coursework, to the point where he had to take a break from university. He suffered through a period of confusion and depression, and is still not sure if he will in fact return to school. It's been a hard time for my family, and yet amid the challenges, I have enjoyed the support of my wife and a tightly knit group of friends, one of whom helped my son get a job that allows him to be self-reliant while he decides on next steps. My life isn't "perfect," and yet each morning I wake to a choice–how can I embrace what is good in this day? How can I tap into God within me, no matter what else transpires?

Lord, help me remember that external circumstances cannot define my joy. Rather, joy is something I can nurture within, even as I, and those I love, experience ups and downs.

A merry heart doeth good like a medicine: but a broken spirit drieth the bones.

–Proverbs 17:22

Last summer I started bicycling regularly for my health. One day late in August I jumped a curb too exuberantly, wiped out, and broke my leg. Fortunately, I work from home, so my schedule was not too affected during my recuperation time. And yet, because I am by nature an active person, the limitations of my injury–not to mention the bulky cast–put a real cramp in my style. I'll confess that some days I felt down. My good friends Dave and Sara were a lifeline during this time. They'd stop by to watch movies, bring in dinner, or just "hang out." We laughed a lot during these visits and I invariably found that after they looked in on me, my mood soared and I felt better overall. Long after my leg has healed, I remember their kindness with gratitude.

Lord, thank you for the friends and loved ones who uplift me. Just as exercise, being joyful is good for my health!

Which when they had read, they rejoiced for the consolation.

–Acts 15:31

In an age of digital, Todd still writes letters to send by post. He writes to his brother. He writes to a favorite uncle. "Sure, I use email, too," he shares. "And I text. But I know I'm always thrilled when I get a 'real' letter in my mailbox, rather than just bills and junk mail. There is permanence to a written note, on lovely paper, that gives me a lift. I hope my letters bring the same kind of joy."

Dear Lord, written words have lasting power. May what I write bring solace and joy!

> *Hitherto have ye asked nothing in my name: ask, and ye shall receive, that your joy may be full.*
>
> –John 16:24

Being an adult—perhaps more specifically being a spiritual adult—does not mean that we have to be dull or unadventurous. I was recently, happily reminded of this fact when I met a woman at my church who embodies the spirit of adventure. Like me, Liz is probably in her late 50s. Like me, she lost her spouse to terminal illness. I have admittedly become stuck in my ways since becoming a widower five years ago. Meeting Liz has been like a shot of sunshine. She is taking lessons to earn a motorcycle license. She loves working in clay and has sold her pottery at local craft fairs. Though she still holds down a full-time job, Liz enjoys volunteering at a nearby animal shelter, an effort that has brought two sleek and satisfied tabby cats into her life. I don't know where our friendship will lead, but I can say that my relationship with Liz has broadened my horizons and filled me with joy.

God, thank you for reminding me that you want us to be happy.

Lord, you are the source of all joy! Regardless of how happy we may feel at any given time, we know happiness is fleeting. Happiness, so dependent on temporary circumstances, is fickle and unpredictable. But joy in you is forever! And so we come to you today, Lord, rejoicing in all you were, all you are, and all you will ever be. Because of you, we rejoice!

Joy is the echo of God's life within us.

–Columba Marmion

O let the nations be glad and sing for joy: for thou shalt judge the people righteously, and govern the nations upon earth.

—Psalm 67:4

Heavenly Father, when I stop for a moment and just think about all the blessings you've showered on me, I'm filled with joy and happiness. I often complain about my problems and focus on the things I wish I had, but in these quiet moments I truly become aware of just how few problems I do have and how much you've given me. Thank you for slowing down my often hectic and crazy life every now and then so I can recognize these moments of pure joy.

For verily I say unto you, That whosoever shall say unto this mountain, Be thou removed, and be thou cast into the sea; and shall not doubt in his heart, but shall believe that those things which he saith shall come to pass; he shall have whatsoever he saith.

–Mark 11:22–23

Heavenly Father, what can be more joyful than to realize that through you, all things are possible? Even when I'm at the lowest point in my life, I only have to reach out to you, and you take me and lift me up again. Though there is much trouble and hardship in my life right now, my joy is knowing that you have reserved a place for me in your heavenly kingdom. Thank you, Father.

These things have I spoken unto you, that my joy might remain in you, and that your joy might be full.

—John 15:11

Young children have a particularly deep capacity for joy. They love fiercely and play hard; their worldview is often one of opportunity and abundance. As we grow, experiences good and bad accrue. We take on more responsibility, for others and for ourselves, and can lose sight of that deep well of joy. It's still there, if we are mindful. But joy is tricky in that it can manifest itself in opposites: there is joy in community, even as it exists in solitary pursuits. A gorgeous summer sky brings joy, as does a brooding landscape. Sometimes we don't recognize joy, but it is there: we can still access it, whether it feels like good loneliness, hilarity, or a deep stillness. It is a gift we must not lose sight of.

Dear Lord, thank you for joy, which comes from you.

For his anger endureth but a moment; in his favour is life: weeping may endure for a night, but joy cometh in the morning.

–Psalm 30:5

Joy will always return to those who love God. We may find ourselves brought low by some of life's difficulties—and certainly by the tragedies that take us by storm. But none of these—not even the tragedies—can rob us of the deep-seated joy we have in our God. We may weep, even as Jesus did at times, but like him, we have a future joy set before us that no struggle on this earth can undermine or destroy. Our morning lies just ahead.

CHAPTER 18

SELF-IMPROVEMENT

And be not conformed to this world: but be ye transformed by the renewing of your mind, that ye may prove what is that good, and acceptable, and perfect, will of God.

–Romans 12:2

The Lord is not slack concerning his promise, as some men count slackness; but is longsuffering to us-ward, not willing that any should perish, but that all should come to repentance.

–2 Peter 3:9

Two steps forward, one step back. My mom, a physical therapist, sometimes says this to clients who feel discouraged about the long road to recovery. "But you'll get there," she always adds. Mom is a spiritual person, and she shared with me once that not only does she think her maxim applies to any process of self-improvement, it reminds her of God's faith in us. I was deeply struck by her observation! Self-improvement is a long haul, marked by setbacks and detours. And yet, God, you always are patient with me, and believe that I can better myself. Thank you for believing in my potential and efforts; I am bolstered by your patience and love.

Therefore if any man be in Christ, he is a new creature: old things are passed away; behold, all things are become new.

–2 Corinthians 5:17

When I was a boy, my favorite uncle used to take me fishing on summer evenings when he was in town. Uncle Will was a truck driver, a job that frequently took him away from his family and friends for days at a time, and he formed some bad habits eating alone on the road. Perhaps not surprisingly, after a number of years of this, my uncle developed diabetes and high blood pressure. Will's doctor warned that his eating habits were going to kill him—a serious wake-up call that prompted some life changes. I still remember the evening my uncle and I were out on the river, hoping to catch a pike but mostly reeling in bluegills; he told me it was through God's grace that he was able to change his ways. "I'm healthier," Uncle Will said when I complimented his weight loss. And then he added something I've never forgotten: "God didn't just help me get better, he transformed me. Not just on the outside. On the inside."

Lord, you are there to help us better ourselves, not just externally, but internally. Thank you for being there.

Thy word is a lamp unto my feet, and a light unto my path.

–Psalm 119:105

As a college student living in the United States, I have many advantages, and it's easy to fall into the trap of feeling that, given all I have going for me, I should "be the best at everything." I am hard on myself when I don't get the best grade, for example, or when I perceive that I'm not as physically fit as some of my dorm mates.

God, help me to remember that there is always room for improvement, a condition I share with everyone else on Earth, and that your Word can comfort me, guide me, and serve as the ultimate "self-improvement manual."

But grow in grace, and in the knowledge of our Lord and Saviour Jesus Christ. To him be glory both now and for ever. Amen.

–2 Peter 3:18

I have a temper, Ted admits; his short fuse is something he has worked on for much of his life. "I'd been making progress, but then my son Greg turned 15 and we started butting heads all the time!" he shares. "I was discouraged by the setback, but I'm trying hard to respond to Greg in a different, more positive way. With God's help, I know I can continue to grow: as a parent, and as a person."

God, I am a work in progress, and with your help I will continue to grow. Help me to face setbacks in my personal evolution with courage and good humor.

Let your light so shine before men, that they may see your good works, and glorify your Father which is in heaven.

—Matthew 5:16

I am by nature a quiet and reserved person; like my parents before me, I've always believed actions speak louder than words. When our pastor recently gave a sermon challenging the congregation to go out and share with others the way God has helped us grow, I initially felt resistant. "Not my style!" was my kneejerk reaction. And yet talking with the pastor after the service, I realized that showing reverence to God could take different forms. I don't have to go out and preach about how God has helped me improve myself. I can simply demonstrate growth through my actions, whether I'm quitting smoking or getting better at managing my temper. If people ask, as someone recently did, "How did you quit smoking?" I can always give a simple answer: "Prayer."

Lord, I can demonstrate my beliefs and inspire others by always striving to better myself. Please help me to honor you in this way.

And we know that all things work together for good to them that love God, to them who are the called according to his purpose.

—Romans 8:28

Sometimes I get discouraged! Miles says with a laugh. He's talking about his efforts to be more organized at work. "My desk still gets really messy sometimes—I'm terrible about filing things away and I get these piles of paper everywhere—but I remind myself that I'm on the right path. My performance at work has improved overall." He smiles wryly. "There is hope!"

Dear Lord, help me to have confidence that I am on the right path as I strive to grow as a person.

Be not deceived: evil communications corrupt good manners.

—1 Corinthians 15:33

I appreciate the connections made possible by social media, but I also recognize that like everything else, when it comes to technology, moderation is key. Yesterday I was glued to a series of screens throughout the day, from phone to laptop, and when I tore myself away to make dinner, I found myself in a particularly ill humor. While I had happily corresponded with an old friend who lives on another continent, I'd also witnessed a good deal of negativity, judgmental attitudes, and blatantly hateful behavior online. The prolonged exposure had soured my spirit, and when I snapped at my son, I realized that my choices that day did not benefit my family or me.

God, help me to capitalize on the good inherent in technology, while also practicing moderation and sound judgment. Do not let me fall prey to the negativity that can be part of the online experience.

There is much to drag us back, O Lord: empty pursuits, trivial pleasures, unworthy cares. There is much to frighten us away: pride that makes us reluctant to accept help; cowardice that recoils from sharing your suffering; anguish at the prospect of confessing our sins to you. But you are stronger than all these forces. We call you our redeemer and saviour because you redeem us from our empty, trivial existence, you save us from our foolish fears. This is your work, which you have completed and will continue to complete every moment.

—Søren Kierkegaard

My son, despise not the chastening of the Lord; neither be weary of his correction: For whom the Lord loveth he correcteth; even as a father the son in whom he delighteth.

–Proverbs 3:11-12

Lord, correct me today. I know you want to curb my bad habits and improve my better ones. Sometimes you do this by letting me fail or suffer. Sometimes you do it not giving me what I want or sitting me in a quiet place. Help me not to be weary of your work. I know you love me and want the best for me. Thank you, Lord, for your correction.

But Jesus beheld them, and said unto them, With men this is impossible; but with God all things are possible.

—Matthew 19:26

I have always been a social drinker. Shy by nature, having a beer helps me relax and feel more comfortable in social settings. But lately I've noticed that I've begun to rely on a drink to unwind after work, or to gear up for a stressful encounter. When I made the decision to cut back, I was surprised and dismayed to discover how dependent I've become on alcohol to fill an emotional need. I think the best path for me is abstinence. Now that I no longer can rely on alcohol to "take off the edge," each day is a struggle.

Lord, please give me the strength to persevere in eschewing alcohol. I know my health and well-being will benefit. I thank you for your grace.

Put on therefore, as the elect of God, holy and beloved, bowels of mercies, kindness, humbleness of mind, meekness, longsuffering.

–Colossians 3:12

Teach me, teach me, dearest Jesus
In thine own sweet loving, way,
All the lessons of perfection
I must practice day by day.
Teach me meekness, dearest Jesus,
Of thine own the counterpart;
Not in words and actions only,
But the meekness of the heart.
Teach, humility sweet Jesus
To this poor, proud heart of mine,
Which yet wishes, O my Jesus,
To be modeled after thine.

–Reverend F. X. Lasance

Then spake Jesus again unto them, saying, I am the light of the world: he that followeth me shall not walk in darkness, but shall have the light of life.

–John 8:12

There's a path straddling the Montana-Idaho border—an old railroad bed that's been converted into a "rail trail" for bicycles. This fifteen-mile stretch is touted as "one of the most breathtaking scenic stretches of railroad in the country," with seven high spans and ten tunnels. One of these tunnels stretches for nearly two miles. Without a bicycle light, it would be virtually impossible to ride through without falling or crashing. A lightless rider's best hope would be to find another rider with a light and ride very close to that individual. Life, too, is beautiful in places, but it can also be treacherous. The best way to make it through is by staying close to Jesus, the light of the world.

Therefore, my beloved brethren, be ye stedfast, unmoveable, always abounding in the work of the Lord, forasmuch as ye know that your labour is not in vain in the Lord.

–1 Corinthians 15:58

I recently changed jobs. For many years, I'd worked in a medical office and for most of the time, the pros of that situation outweighed the cons. I enjoyed flexible hours, a Godsend when my elderly father grew ill and needed more help. But my boss was never supportive and the pay was not ideal. When my dad passed away last year, I decided to look for a different position, and almost immediately found a new job. I am excited about this next chapter, but change can also be hard: during these first weeks at work, the learning curve has been steep and some nights I am tired and stressed.

Dear God, please help me to remain steadfast as I seek to learn, grow, and improve my situation and myself. Please remind me, on the days when my spirit flags, that you are always there.

CHAPTER 19
GRATITUDE

Every good gift and every perfect gift is from above, and cometh down from the Father of lights, with whom is no variableness, neither shadow of turning.

–James 1:17

O give thanks unto the Lord; for he is good: for his mercy endureth for ever.

—Psalm 136:1

My son Tad is three, and he can be sweet one moment, then overcome by storms of temper the next. The other day, he was tired and had a meltdown when I asked him to put away his toys before dinner. As a parent, I am not always as even-tempered as I should be. But this was one of those times when I had the patience to do it right. I drew Tad onto my lap and rocked him until he calmed down. As my son and I sat together, looking out at the quiet evening street, I thought of God's patience when I rail against the storms of life.

Lord, I am grateful to you because you are always good and merciful to me.

> *Wherefore we receiving a kingdom which cannot be moved, let us have grace, whereby we may serve God acceptably with reverence and godly fear.*
>
> –Hebrews 12:28

I attend church regularly, but I find that the place I feel closest to God is in nature. My home backs up to a forest preserve, and whenever I can, I try to hike the trails there. As I walk through these trees, which existed before I was born and will stand tall long after my death, I am reminded of God's permanence. I am at an age when some of my friends are facing real limitations due to health issues, and slowly they are passing away. But being in the woods lifts my heart as I am surrounded by leafy evidence that God's presence is everlasting. During my walks, I have my best conversations with God. I talk to him about how grateful I am for the life he has given me and that I am still healthy enough to hike, fast and for great distance. I am also grateful that when my time on Earth is finally done, I will move on to a place where I will abide permanently in God's grace and love. God's natural creation is but a taste of what is to come.

Lord, thank you for recognizing the gratitude that underlies my simple and perhaps unconventional worship in the woods.

In every thing give thanks: for this is the will of God in Christ Jesus concerning you.

–1 Thessalonians 5:18

It's been a challenging year. I work in a volatile industry, and was laid off after my company merged with another. The layoff came as a surprise, and at a time when my wife and I have been hit with some unexpected expenses, chiefly for home maintenance as we deal with an old roof and an older furnace. And yet, there are blessings. My company gave me a generous severance, which allows me time to figure out next steps for my career without panicking. We have savings that will help us finance the new roof, and I am reminded to be grateful that we have a roof over our heads! Ours is a happy home, filled with children and pets, books and music and sunlight.

Dear Lord, even in hard times, there is always something for which I can be grateful.

This is the day which the Lord hath made; we will rejoice and be glad in it.

–Psalm 118:24

Earlier this week I took it upon myself to visit a local botanic garden. It is just minutes from my home, but I don't often think to go there. I went on a weekday this time, which meant that the park was much less crowded. I appreciated the solitude, and chose to walk a path that winds around a small lake and through pinewoods. The path is made of wood chips, and as I rounded a bend, I heard a crunching noise, as if someone else were walking and enjoying the bright day. I expected to encounter another hiker. Imagine my surprise when I instead found myself face to face with a deer! The doe looked at me with clear brown eyes, unafraid, and I tried to remain perfectly still. I do not think I exaggerate when I say that we shared a moment; then she regained herself and bounded away. I am so glad I made the effort to visit the botanic garden that day!

Dear Lord, thank you for an encounter that filled my spirit. Thank you for this world.

Lord, behold our family here assembled. We thank you this place in which we dwell, for the love that unites us, for the peace accorded us this day, for the hope with which we expect the morrow; for the health, the work, the food and the bright skies that make our lives delightful; for our friends in all parts of the earth. Amen.

–Robert Louis Stevenson

Heavenly Father, we are thankful for family. Please bring our family together in happiness. Help us see everything as your children do: with wonder and awe. Glorious are your creations! Thank you for creating us. We love our family. We love you. Amen.

And whatsoever ye do in word or deed, do all in the name of the Lord Jesus, giving thanks to God and the Father by him.

–Colossians 3:17

Some days are joyful. Yesterday was such a day. I attended church, it was a good sermon, and as the pastor led us in prayer, my thankfulness sprang forth easily. It felt good to thank you, God. When I walked out into the world, it was as though I was smiling and the world smiled back at me. At lunch I swapped jokes with our waitress and thanked her by leaving a good tip. When we stopped by the nursing home where my dad lives, I appreciated the time I was able to spend laughing and talking with some of the residents. One older gentleman who served in World War II relayed a story about his experiences, and I thanked him for sharing. "You are a happy person," he commented. "I can tell by your gratitude." I was deeply touched by his statement, and reminded that showing appreciation to others, not only in words but in actions, is one way of passing on the thankfulness we feel in our own hearts.

Dear Lord, help me to always give thanks to you in the way I conduct myself.

Happy is that people, that is in such a case: yea, happy is that people, whose God is the Lord.

–Psalm 144:15

God, how long have I looked outside of myself for the blessings that were waiting all along? How often have I complained to you about life not being the way I wanted it when I already had what I needed to change? I now know that the blessings of prosperity and joy are all an inside job. By turning first to you, dear God, all else is then opened before me. You taught that your kingdom was within, not without, and yet once we recognized it, we would also see it all around us.
Thank you, God.

Even every one that is called by my name: for I have created him for my glory, I have formed him; yea, I have made him.

–Isaiah 43:7

When Andrew's son Keith left for college, Andrew was surprised to discover the extent to which he felt at loose ends. "I was still working as a mechanic then," he remembers, "but with Keith successfully out in the world, I felt a lack of motivation." Reexamining his faith helped. "I began by thanking God for Keith's happiness–the way he was spreading his wings," Andrew says now. "Glorifying God in this way restored to me a feeling of purpose."

God, when I'm feeling down about myself and my purpose in life, may I remember to glorify you–that is my purpose!

To the end that my glory may sing praise to thee, and not be silent. O Lord my God, I will give thanks unto thee for ever.

–Psalm 30:12

Lord, so often it isn't until after a crisis has passed that we can see all the ways that you were present in the midst of it. Forgive us for focusing on the negative and missing your positive contributions. Remind us to expect your involvement–to actively watch for it, even! We need to be alert to the working of your Spirit in all things and give thanks at all times.

And I will make them and the places round about my hill a blessing; and I will cause the shower to come down in his season; there shall be showers of blessing.

—Ezekiel 34:26

Lord, my heart overflows with gratitude for all the blessings you have sent into my life. I am cognizant of the fact that I am probably only aware of a small percentage of them, though. You are such a generous God; you shower us with such abundance. I am grateful for it all, Lord.

Forgive me for complaining, dear God. Help me to remember that every time I have a headache, someone I know may have a hidden heartache; every time I don't like the food, millions have nothing to eat; every time I think my paycheck is small, too many people have no paycheck at all; every time I wish my loved ones were not so demanding, some people have no one to love. When I look around at my blessings, my complaints seem little. Teach me perspective, God, and to be grateful for my everyday gifts of family, food, and home. Amen.

Count your blessings, name them one by one: Count your blessings, see what God hath done.

–Johnson Oatman, Jr.

CHAPTER 20
COMPASSION

Finally, be ye all of one mind, having compassion one of another, love as brethren, be pitiful, be courteous.

–1 Peter 3:8

> *Then the lord of that servant was moved with compassion, and loosed him, and forgave him the debt.*
>
> –Matthew 18:27

God, I aspire to be the person you want me to be, to live the life you want for me, but sometimes I struggle. I have a friend to whom I lent money; it has become apparent that not only will he not be able to repay what he owes, but he has also been avoiding me. I caught sight of him in town yesterday, and he literally crossed the street to avoid any interaction. Even when I called out to him, he would not meet my eye. I know he is ashamed that he cannot repay me, but I'm disappointed in him. I wish I'd never lent him the money. Please grant me the compassion and grace to forgive this debt, and move on.

Therefore his sisters sent unto him, saying, Lord, behold, he whom thou lovest is sick.

–John 11:3

I move through my days with a sense of purpose, but sometimes I am so consumed by the immediate to-dos that I forget to be open to—or even aware of—opportunities for compassion. This week was no exception. My mind has been on a tight work deadline, and at night, I've been tackling a series of home repairs. It was only when my wife sat me down and made me put my phone aside that I slowed down long enough for her to share that a close friend of ours has been battling depression. If I'd been paying attention, I might have seen the signals. This friend is usually good about staying in touch, but I hadn't heard from him in several months. "Why don't you give him a call?" was my wife's gentle suggestion.

God, help me to be sensitive to those I love, and those in need. Jesus was responsive when he learned that Lazarus was sick; may I likewise show compassion.

He that oppresseth the poor reproacheth his Maker: but he that honoureth him hath mercy on the poor.

–Proverbs 14:31

I long to help every needy person in the world, Lord. Perhaps the most effective way to do this is by praying that you will send help wherever it is needed. Meanwhile, there is my corner of the universe with its many needs, and some of these are surely within my reach: half of my sandwich to the person standing near the freeway ramp with a sign; an evening spent going through my closet and setting aside items to donate; a weekend afternoon of helping with events at my church; a monthly visit to the sick, homebound, or imprisoned. It's a privilege to honor you by extending your compassion–in person.

And Saul said, Blessed be ye of the Lord; for ye have compassion on me.

–1 Samuel 23:21

My kindergarten-age daughter has had a "best friend" since preschool, but recently the other little girl has been unkind to my daughter, pointedly excluding her at recess and talking about her unkindly to the other girls in their class. After more than a month of this behavior, my wife spoke to the other girl's mother, and the woman was defensive, even hostile, intimating that it was our daughter's fault and that she was provoking her child in some way. My wife gently persisted, and as we talked to the other family and our own child, it became apparent that the other little girl is jealous of our daughter's reading ability. Though it helped to understand the situation, matters haven't changed much between the girls. We have alerted the teacher to the situation, and encouraged our daughter to seek other playmates. She's made the adjustment, but my wife and I were disappointed at the hostility the other mother showed us, and her unwillingness to hold her own daughter accountable.

Dear Lord, help me to feel (and demonstrate) compassion for this family, even if they do not respond in kind, and even as I am an advocate for my child. Please help me to proceed with grace.

But thou, O Lord, art a God full of compassion, and gracious, long suffering, and plenteous in mercy and truth.

–Psalm 86:15

It is easy to be judgmental. It is easy to write another person off when they fall short of our expectations. Even those we love will disappoint us. Yesterday I was short with my sister when she called to let me know that she won't be able to take our mother shopping this weekend. I was counting on her help, and at first, I wouldn't let myself hear her explanation: her own daughter is sick, and her husband, my brother-in-law, has been pulling extra shifts at work. It took effort for me to overcome my own annoyance and listen to what she had to say.

Dear Lord, help me to remember that compassion comes from you. May I be inspired by the compassion you show me every day, and may I in turn show compassion to others.

And when she had opened it, she saw the child: and, behold, the babe wept. And she had compassion on him, and said, This is one of the Hebrews' children.

–Exodus 2:6

My wife and I, unable to bear a child of our own, have recently begun thinking about adoption. The thought of helping a parentless child is meaningful to us, and we've started investigating what it might mean to adopt a child. Our friends recently adopted a little girl, and their journey and the joy they've experienced fill us with hope. We know we have a lot of love to give. And how expanding our little family would enrich our lives!

God, please guide us as we endeavor to reach out to a child in need. Please keep us humble and cognizant of how much we stand to gain by showing compassion to another.

Thus speaketh the Lord of hosts, saying, Execute true judgment, and shew mercy and compassions every man to his brother.

—Zechariah 7:9

We live in an information society. Daily, we are bombarded with news. Our phones, televisions, and laptops keep us breathlessly apprised of the latest events. It is good to be informed, and technology is a gift. But an adverse effect of all-information-all-the-time is a sort of numbing of the senses. "Another earthquake?" we shrug. "Another tragedy?" It can be an effort to dig deep and access caring, and yet compassion is a Godly virtue. God wants us to experience concern for the sufferings of others.

Dear Lord, help us to strike a balance in our information intake so that we retain compassion for those in need. May we never become callous to others' misfortune.

Bless the Lord, O my soul, and forget not all his benefits: Who forgiveth all thine iniquities; who healeth all thy diseases; Who redeemeth thy life from destruction; who crowneth thee with loving-kindness and tender mercies.

–Psalm 103:2–4

Today I thank you for medical professionals: doctors and nurses and technicians. I ask you to bless them, to give them the gift of being compassionate with their patients, to help them say the right words when breaking bad news. I ask you to protect and shield them from burnout, that they have the support they need in their own lives to heal from the difficult times they go through. Please help them know that you are always with them, Our Great Physician.

It is of the Lord's mercies that we are not consumed, because his compassions fail not. They are new every morning: great is thy faithfulness.

—Lamentations 3:22–23

Let me wake up each morning determined to see your presence in my life. Let me focus throughout the day not on what I don't have, but the blessings you give me so abundantly. It's easy for me to become distracted from your presence during the course of the day—but when I look, I see your mercy and compassion at work in my life.

A soft answer turneth away wrath: but grievous words stir up anger.

—Proverbs 15:1

My sister Emma and I are like night and day: even though we grew up in the same house, and were raised by the same parents, our worldviews are strikingly different. We've had different ideas about how to help our aging parents, and we have different ideas on how to be a parent. And though we love each other, we don't always get along. Yesterday Emma criticized the way I'm handling a conflict with a mutual friend, and I had to bite my tongue to keep from lashing out. I managed to respond with a joke, and it was amazing, how the tension between us drained away.

God, help me to remember: when in a quarrel, I must have compassion and strive to take the high road. A soft answer can diffuse an argument before it begins.